"Details practical steps that are not only effective but essential to help protect and ensure the wellness of those who serve. This book is a must-read for all first responders."

— **Shelley Zimmerman**, Chief of Police (ret.),
San Diego Police Department

"The book tells you why you might be traumatized by any number of criminal or emergency situations, and it offers case studies of events that would be hard to live with in the minds of even the strongest personalities. And then it brings suggestions, guidelines, and resolutions to help us live with the problems, crises, and destructions which we see every day in the lives of others."

— **Dennis Smith**,
author of *Report from Ground Zero*

"Captain Willis has written a practical, extremely useful, and important guide for first responders everywhere....This book offers the essential keys for preparation for, protection from, and healing after trauma for all those devoted to public safety."

— **Catherine Butler, PhD, EdD, MFT**,
psychologist to emergency first responders

"[Captain Willis's] work emphasizes the significance of wellness encompassing the mind, body, and spirit, and he reminds us that it is vital not only to nurture but to be nurtured as well."

— **Bobby Smith, PhD**, former Louisiana State Trooper
and author of *Visions of Courage* and *The Will to Survive*

"Exposes the silent dangers, and sometimes killers, of many of our first-responder heroes in a dynamic and compassionate way...It *will* save lives."

— **Clarke Paris**, Las Vegas Metro police sergeant (ret.),
author of *My Life for Your Life*, president of
The Pain Behind the Badge Training LLC

"This book would be a valuable asset to any first responder, clinician, or peer-support person working with first responders."

— **Kevin Gilmartin, PhD**, author of
Emotional Survival for Law Enforcement

POLICE RESILIENCE

Also by Dan Willis

Bulletproof Spirit:
The First Responder's Essential Resource
for Protecting and Healing Mind and Heart

Required reading for wellness courses at the FBI National Academy

POLICE RESILIENCE

Bulletproof Spirit Wellness Strategies for Training Academies and New Peace Officers

Captain Dan Willis (ret.)

International instructor on peace officer trauma, wellness, and resilience

*International Academy of Public Safety
National Command and Staff College*

New World Library
Novato, California

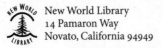

New World Library
14 Pamaron Way
Novato, California 94949

Parts of this book appeared previously in *Bulletproof Spirit*, revised edition © 2014, 2019 by Dan Willis.

Grateful acknowledgment is made to Julia Holladay for permission to include the results of her study in conjunction with the San Diego Police Department.

Text design by Tona Pearce Myers

Library of Congress Cataloging-in-Publication Data

Names: Willis, Dan, date, author.
Title: Police resilience : bulletproof spirit wellness strategies for training academies and new peace officers / Captain Dan Willis (ret.), International Instructor on peace officer trauma, wellness, and resilience, International Academy of Public Safety, National Command and Staff College.
Description: Novato, California : New World Library, [2022] | Includes bibliographical references. | Summary: "A former police captain and SWAT commander describes a range of techniques designed to help police officers and other first responders maintain their psychological well-being on the job. The book includes case studies, personal stories from officers, questions for reflection, and links to informative videos"-- Provided by publisher.
Identifiers: LCCN 2022018699 (print) | LCCN 2022018700 (ebook) | ISBN 9781608688203 (paperback) | ISBN 9781608688210 (epub)
Subjects: LCSH: Police psychology. | Resilience (Personality trait)
Classification: LCC HV7936.P75 W55 2022 (print) | LCC HV7936.P75 (ebook) | DDC 363.201/9--dc23/eng/20220425
LC record available at https://lccn.loc.gov/2022018699
LC ebook record available at https://lccn.loc.gov/2022018700

First printing, August 2022
ISBN 978-1-60868-820-3
Ebook ISBN 978-1-60868-821-0
Printed in Canada on 100% postconsumer-waste recycled paper

New World Library is proud to be a Gold Certified Environmentally Responsible Publisher. Publisher certification awarded by Green Press Initiative.

10   9   8   7   6   5   4   3   2   1

*We shall draw from the heart of suffering itself
the means of inspiration and survival.*
— WINSTON CHURCHILL

Contents

---★---

Introduction

*The purpose of human life is to serve and to show
compassion and the will to help others.*
— ALBERT SCHWEITZER

As a peace officer, if you are not driven by your heart to make a positive difference with every call and to do as much good as you can for your colleagues, your agency, and your community in compassionate and meaningful ways, then the job can eat you alive.

Consistent exposure to violence, daily work traumas, suffering, danger, and death can scar a first responder's spirit and take a terrible toll. Suicide, posttraumatic stress, diseases and other serious health problems, addictions, sleep disorders, indifference, depression, alcoholism, broken relationships, emotional suffering, and lost careers plague this honored profession. Yet much of this is preventable through the daily practice of wellness and resilience strategies.

On average, about 130 officers commit suicide annually,

which is the number one cause of death for peace officers —
typically more than all the other causes of death combined. I'm
sure, at the beginning of their careers, these officers thought
the same thing most of us do: *There is absolutely nothing that
could ever happen to cause me to take my own life. I have far too
much to live for.* Yet that's the horrific power of accumulated
trauma. It can cause someone to lose hope, to feel helpless, and
to suffer unimaginable emotional and psychological distress.
In other words, the daily work traumas that come with this job
not only cause a range of mental and physical injuries, *they can
kill you.*

Up to 19 percent of peace officers will suffer severe posttraumatic stress during their career, which currently equals
about 120,000 officers. Peace officers are twice as likely to
become alcoholics; 40 percent have serious sleep disorders;
20 percent will develop a serious addiction; and 25 to 30 percent will have at least one serious stress-based health problem
during their career. My hope is that this wellness guide can help
you avoid becoming one of these statistics. It provides science-
and evidence-based resilience strategies that are a proven path
to manifesting optimal wellness. Ours is a noble profession,
but unless we take control of our physical, mental, emotional,
and spiritual fitness, it can exact a steep cost.

I've devoted my entire adult life to public safety. I was a
police officer for thirty years, and I have also trained over seven
thousand officers throughout North America on how to protect themselves and heal from the effects of daily work traumas. I truly wish I had had a wellness and resilience guidebook
like this when I started my career; it would have saved me from
much suffering and heartache.

My goal is to help you so hopefully you won't struggle in

the ways I did. I want you to be successful and to have the most meaningful and fulfilling career possible. I want you to remain motivated and inspired throughout your entire career to do as much good as you can by protecting lives and serving others. I want you to thrive and to thoroughly enjoy and love this wonderful profession. But achieving that requires developing *daily* wellness strategies that continually strengthen your resilience in mind, body, emotions, and spirit.

As a twenty-one-year-old in the police academy, I was filled with idealism. I wanted to protect life and to serve my country, my community, and those in need. I had no idea that every traumatic call I would experience over the next thirty years would slowly eat away at, not only my idealism, but my ability and desire to want to make a difference. I suffered in many ways: divorce, indifference, inability to sleep, symptoms of posttraumatic stress, and becoming emotionally dead inside.

Over the course of my police career, I was a crimes of violence, sexual assault, child molestation, and homicide detective; a SWAT commander; a wellness unit and peer support director; a sergeant, lieutenant, and captain. As a lieutenant, I attended the FBI National Academy, where for ten weeks I studied emotional survival and wellness strategies from their Behavioral Science Unit. That led me to various experiences that significantly changed my career and in many ways changed my life — and what I learned is what I want to share with you in this book.

It's essential that you begin your career with your eyes wide open. The daily work traumas of this profession have the potential to change you into someone your loved ones don't recognize anymore — into someone you may not even recognize. Without ongoing, daily wellness and resilience practices, these traumas can be crippling. They can erode your quality of life and undermine your ability to be there for your family — and for all those you love who need and depend upon you.

I know firsthand the suffering our profession can cause. I've experienced intense emotional and psychological distress throughout my career. I've been falsely accused of terrible things numerous times. I've been shot at, assaulted, threatened, surveilled, and followed by accomplices of sadistic murderers who had cut off someone's head and hands. I know officers who have committed suicide, who have been murdered, and who have never mentally or emotionally recovered from the work traumas they've experienced.

Nevertheless, I also know firsthand that there is hope. I know that if you practice daily the numerous proactive wellness strategies in this guide, they will help protect you from these negative outcomes. They will enhance your resilience, sustain your motivation, improve your ability to respond constructively to traumas and challenges, and increase wellness. These strategies will help keep you safe so that you may serve others in the way you intend.

Public safety is the foundation of a free, safe, and prosperous society. There is no nobler profession than that of a peace officer devoted to protecting and enabling life. There is great honor in being the good amidst the bad; in serving and helping people; and in being willing to sacrifice a part of oneself to prevent crime, restore justice, and keep the peace.

However, never imagine that traumatic incidents are something that you should get used to and not be bothered by. Becoming an officer doesn't keep you from being human, someone who fears, suffers, and bleeds like everyone else. Always remember that it's okay to be human. It's okay to be sickened or extremely troubled by certain experiences. In fact, it's critical to recognize these reactions when they arise and address them. Ultimately, what is most destructive is when an officer buries those experiences and pretends they're not affected. Maybe they feel that admitting being affected by trauma is a sign of weakness or indicates that there is something wrong with them. But when we recognize when we have been injured by an experience, that allows us to identify effective ways to recover and heal.

It's important to emphasize that our brains and our central nervous system never get used to traumatic experiences. They are instead injured by them, and when these injuries are left untreated, the effect can be like a cancer that slowly eats away at our ability to be normal. Many people, not just officers, wait until they are desperate before seeking help, and that only makes treatment that much harder and more difficult. *Don't wait to be in crisis before taking the inevitable traumas of work seriously.*

The purpose of this wellness and resilience guidebook is to enable you to serve honorably, to do tremendous good throughout your career, and to reach retirement healthy and well. My hope is that you will look back upon your career in retirement full of pride and thankful that you were able to protect and positively affect countless lives.

For thirty years, despite all the traumas I experienced on the job, I looked forward to going to work every day. That's how I *know* these strategies work. I absolutely loved police work, and I still miss it every day. I am filled with peace and am well.

May you experience all the peace, joy, and fulfillment that a professional life of compassionate service has to offer.

Chapter One

—————————— ★ ——————————

Trauma, Wellness, and Resilience

When we are no longer able to change a situation,
we are challenged to change ourselves.
— VIKTOR E. FRANKL

Becoming a peace officer is an honor that comes with immense responsibilities, difficulties, and heartache. The work can be exciting, thrilling, intense, fun, fulfilling, exhausting, challenging, and dangerous. Our nation's freedom and the safety of our communities depend upon us — and how successfully we do our job depends upon how well we mitigate the effects of trauma while enhancing our wellness and resilience. This chapter provides an overview of what these three things — trauma, wellness, and resilience — mean in practice.

Trauma

Trauma is any experience that adversely affects us in a significant way over a long period of time. As a peace officer, you will have numerous traumatic experiences — some major, most less so — throughout your career.

When most peace officers think of trauma, they envision a shooting, a riot, or being violently assaulted. Yet posttraumatic stress can arise just from the day-in, day-out experience of the job. You will experience thousands of lesser traumas throughout your career, and the impacts add up and can injure your brain just as seriously as a major horrific critical incident.

Every experience of trauma can shock and injure the brain, but the effects are also cumulative. If we don't do anything proactively each day to constructively process and move through traumas, big and small, then these effects can build up. These daily traumas can reach the point where our brain becomes overburdened and incapable of processing events and filing them away in our memory. That's the serious injury that is the precursor to posttraumatic stress.

Many peace officers falsely assume that they will simply get used to daily traumas — that these experiences are "just part of the job." Early in their careers, when their resilience is high, they may find their ability to cope despite experiencing trauma proves them right. Yet how many fatal car collisions with mangled corpses; how many child molestation and sexual assault victims; how many fights, threats, and dangerous altercations; how many deranged, psychopathic, and mentally ill people; and how much violence and death can a person encounter before they lose that resilience and become seriously affected? Make no mistake about it. Even when there is no outward, physical injury, every traumatic experience causes internal, emotional, mental, and spiritual injuries in ways we often don't realize. Yet the negative effects of these traumas can be minimized and mitigated.

Over time, accumulated trauma can affect our brain's coping ability, resilience, and ability to function optimally, and so our minds react in certain defensive or negative ways to try to cope. Here are some signs that trauma is causing significant distress within your brain and central nervous system: You experience intrusive and disturbing thoughts, uncontrollable emotions, anger, rage, depression, despondency, isolation, emotional numbness, unreal visions, panic attacks, inability to sleep, and anxiety. You may feel like you're losing it, that your life is spiraling out of control, or even that you're losing your mind. Typically, when these reactions occur, we are not even consciously aware of the cause. We don't associate them with work or a particular incident.

Other signs of negative coping are that you become uncaring and indifferent, disengaged with life, and uninvolved with interests and people. You overreact to minor annoyances; find it hard to think clearly and rationally; act unprofessionally with others or use excessive force; and lose interest in life, relationships, and work.

No one is impervious to the corrosive effects of trauma. The more we try to pretend that our work traumas don't affect us, the more vulnerable we become to suffering because of them.

The effects of accumulated trauma tend to be slow and insidious — much like a cancer slowly eating away at our ability to be normal, to maintain close meaningful relationships, and to maintain a high quality of life. That's why it's so imperative not to wait until you experience obvious signs of being affected, but to practice wellness and resilience strategies every day to mitigate those effects.

When the brain's processing functions become injured by trauma, our primitive fight-or-flight reactions tend to take over all the time. This is why, even when we're sitting alone on a sofa watching television, we might feel all the fear, panic, terror, anxiety, and emotions that come with being in a dangerous situation. When the brain races continually, our fight-or-flight reactions tend to never turn off.

At the same time, the part of the brain that regulates emotion and enables effective communication tends to shut down. This is why we can feel emotionally numb or dead inside and unable to express emotions or communicate clearly and effectively. We become less able to connect and relate to people.

The part of the brain responsible for rational thought also tends to shut down, which is why we can't concentrate, think clearly, make good decisions, and respond to stress rationally.

This is similar to how, when a computer gets overloaded or doesn't have enough processing power, it slows down or freezes up and won't work properly. The good news is that, like a computer, we can reboot our brains and restore normal functioning, such as by using the numerous wellness and resilience strategies in this book. For me, one of the most effective methods is EMDR, or eye movement desensitization and reprocessing (see "EMDR Therapy," pages 119–122). After two sessions of EMDR, I resolved an issue that bothered me off and on for twenty-five years. However, whatever strategies and techniques you use, the main thing is to be aware of the effects of trauma and to constructively process those reactions to hopefully prevent them from accumulating.

★ "I Have Seen" ★

Throughout *Police Resilience*, I include links to YouTube videos produced specifically for this book. To view them, simply scan the QR codes with your phone.

These videos are primarily of veteran officers and first responders sharing their own experiences and advice.

In the eight-minute video "I Have Seen," several veteran officers describe how their specific trauma experiences dramatically affected them — the same traumas you are very likely to experience as a fellow peace officer. Becoming aware of the traumas and difficult experiences you may encounter is the best way to prepare for them and to limit their potential impact. Take work trauma seriously from the beginning so you can respond in constructive ways that will enhance your resilience and wellness.

https://www.youtube.com/watch?v=__KgcBVpD5w
Courtesy of LegacyProductions.org

★

Wellness

Wellness is the foundation for officer safety. I use the word *wellness* to refer to the entire safety net of practices, attributes, and support that allows officers to not only survive but thrive and be most effective throughout their career. Fostering wellness ensures individual success, agency effectiveness, and positive community impact.

Wellness goes far beyond physical fitness. Wellness involves physical, emotional, mental, and spiritual fitness and resilience. These are the four components that make us human, and all four need to be strengthened and enhanced *daily* because they are interdependent and interrelated with one another.

Physical wellness means being free of illness or injury as well as having strength, stamina, and endurance, which are maintained through consistent exercise. This also involves eating a holistic, well-balanced diet of good, nutritious foods and staying well-hydrated.

Emotional wellness involves being emotionally intelligent. This is fostered through the practice of mindfulness, which means living in the present moment, being aware of our emotions, and being able to feel and express them. This enables us to relate to people and to nurture relationships, to communicate effectively, and to feel joys and fulfillment while remaining positive. Emotional wellness allows us to maintain a healthy work-life balance, which is essential.

Mental fitness refers to the ability to make good decisions and exercise sound judgment, to think clearly and rationally, to be creative, to idealize, and to envision good things. An essential part of achieving this is to cultivate interests and a curiosity about life.

Spiritual wellness enables us to connect with people in deep, meaningful ways. It springs from, or provides, a sense of life purpose and a desire to help others and be useful beyond our own self-interests. Spiritual wellness fosters tolerance, compassion, selflessness, humility, openness to learning, kindness, and mercy. Spiritual wellness enables us to consistently affirm the good in ourselves, to do good for others through heart-centered service, and to live with integrity. Spiritual wellness does not necessarily involve a religious faith, though any faith practice can add to it. Faith can provide coping mechanisms and enable inner peace. Spiritual wellness involves maintaining a connection to our core values and principles while working to expand upon them.

If all someone does to foster wellness is to exercise and work out, then their overall resilience and physical health will significantly falter. Science has shown that a lack of emotional wellness, such as suffering depression or anxieties, can lower the immune system and cause physical illness. Conversely, not being physically fit can cause someone to become depressed and uninvolved with life. Any one of the four wellness areas, if allowed to deteriorate, can negatively impact the others. A lack of mental fitness — such as consistently using bad judgment, failing to consider the consequences of one's actions or not caring about them, or being excessively negative — can cause emotional and physical illnesses. A lack of spiritual wellness — perhaps by committing a moral injury against one's integrity or being unwilling to be useful to others or to serve others with compassion — can lead to a loss of purpose and significance, which in turn affects emotional and mental well-being. However, it's also true that every time we improve wellness in any of these areas, that also helps strengthen and enhance wellness in all the others.

An essential pillar of wellness and resilience is to always be learning, growing, and improving. Whatever you are currently doing to enhance wellness in mind, body, emotions, and spirit, contemplate what more you can do and how to practice these things daily. Throughout your career, seek to expand your daily wellness practices to enhance fitness in all four components. This will significantly improve your chances of making it to retirement and being well. It will also enable you to attain the greatest peace, joy, and fulfillment throughout your career.

★ "A Vision of Wellness" ★

In the six-minute video "A Vision of Wellness," police chiefs and a senior officer describe their visions of what resilience and wellness entail.

https://www.youtube.com/watch?v=G2WJZGcjOjw
Courtesy of LegacyProductions.org

★

Resilience

Resilience is the capacity to recover from and to respond to traumas and challenges in constructive ways that foster wellness.

Traumatic, heart-wrenching, terrible, and sometimes horrific things happen during the careers of every peace officer. That doesn't matter. What truly matters is *how you choose to respond to those traumas and challenges*. How you choose to handle every call for service, every interaction you have throughout your career, every trauma you experience — that's all that matters in the long run. Every call matters and is an opportunity to practice wellness and to strengthen resilience.

First responders who are resilient all have several things in common: They have good social support. They see hits to their careers as challenges and not as crises. They are able to feel and express appreciation for the good in their lives. They consciously look at the glass as being half full instead of half empty. They are positive in their outlook, hopeful, and purposeful. They try to turn a negative experience into something positive and useful for the greater good.

Resilience is not a gift; it is something that is built and strengthened over time. Similar to physical fitness, you can become more resilient and fit if you focus on managing stress in effective ways on a regular basis.

Work traumas eat away at our ability to be resilient. Over the years, if we do not practice resilience to strengthen it, we can tend to overreact, to potentially use excessive and unreasonable force, to have an extremely short fuse, and to automatically react in anger in every situation. I believe that many instances of unreasonable use of force are due, at least in part, to the officer having lost resilience due to past traumas.

A key of resilience lies in fostering hope. For an officer, this means intentionally believing that there is good and that we can do good, even if in the present moment we are the only ones trying to do good. Another essential element of resilience is intentionally training our mind to reframe challenges in positive terms. That means not seeing ourselves as a victim, but as someone inwardly empowered to respond in ways that are helpful and constructive, which hopefully will lead to positive outcomes.

A core pillar of resilience is seeing every challenging moment as happening *for you*. That is, treating each challenge as an opportunity for you to practice coping, to intentionally choose your character, to practice and engage resilience, and to try to learn from your experience in order to help someone else later who is going through the same challenge. If you look at the traumas and challenges of life and work in this way, then every difficult thing, every unfair thing, every traumatic thing, every horrible or negative thing only shows up to make you better.

If you find yourself instinctively reacting to challenges or difficulties by fighting or resisting them, try to look upon them as a teacher who is there to enable greater resilience, growth, and character. Every experience has a silver lining, and we need to learn how to find it and benefit from it. The key to this is our mindset, our outlook, what we believe, and what we look for, because whatever we seek in any given situation, we will find.

★ "The Power of Resiliency" ★

In the five-minute video "The Power of Resiliency," trauma professionals and officers describe what resilience looks like to them, and they describe specific strategies to practice daily to strengthen resilience.

In the video, Carlsbad Police Sergeant Ryan Opeka speaks eloquently about this:

Some of these adverse experiences that I've had, whether it was childhood or throughout my career, Marine Corps experiences, combat experiences, that slow, steady drip of traumatic experiences in law enforcement — after seeking counseling and getting some treatment for some of these things that I've been experiencing — I think one of the biggest takeaways for me is that I've learned how to harness those, for lack of a better term, bad experiences and use that as motivation to do good, and to come out better and stronger and respond to things that I was experiencing in the now with an advantage because I had gone through some terrible things before.

I was a high school wrestler. I did martial arts growing up. I was in jujitsu, judo. And one of the principles is using your opponent's momentum against them and taking the energy that they're putting into the fight and then flipping it around on them. I think through my treatment and my experiences, I've recognized that I could do good with the bad things that are happening [by] constantly trying to use the momentum of a bad experience and flip it around on itself and make it a positive.

https://www.youtube.com/watch?v=A9ZYTi3VCik
Courtesy of LegacyProductions.org

★

Self-Awareness Questions

Think of some of the challenges you've faced, the heartaches and setbacks.

- How did you respond to these difficult challenges?
- Were there other ways you could have responded that might have been more constructive, helpful, or productive of wellness and resilience?
- When have you been able to turn a bad experience into a positive one in the way Sergeant Opeka describes?

Case Study: Avoiding Escalation

Officer Hanson pulls over a car for speeding and approaches the driver's side door. The driver initially refuses to lower the window. After being asked again, the driver lowers the window two inches and, in a belligerent tone, demands to know why the officer stopped him. "Don't you have anything better to do, like beat up somebody? What's your problem?"

Officer Hanson replies, "Please let me see your driver's license, registration, and insurance." The irate driver asks tersely, "Why?"

Officer Hanson immediately snaps and angrily responds, "Because I told you! Get out of the car now and give them to me!"

The driver aggressively throws open the car door and leaps out, confronting the officer and yelling at him. Officer Hanson steps back and calls for immediate cover. When the driver keeps walking forward, Officer Hanson pushes him backward, and a fight ensues. Ultimately, the driver is arrested for delaying and obstructing an officer and for assault.

Case Study Reflection

Consider how Officer Hanson might have responded differently to this uncooperative driver. What could he have done to help avoid escalating this confrontation, which significantly increased the risk of harm to both the officer and the driver?

This scenario highlights a common mistake that, unfortunately, many officers make. Without the daily practice of resilience, officers can lose control under stress, yet becoming angry can be like throwing gas on a fire, which endangers everyone, sometimes with tragic results. This case study high-lights two critical learning objectives that are essential for any peace officer to understand in order to remain safe.

1. *Never* make your job personal. "Because I said so" is never a good response because it personalizes the in-teraction with the subject. This can prompt someone to react defensively and often defiantly, as if the officer is causing the problem, not the person's actions. Every-thing an officer does must be authorized by law, pol-icy, and procedure as well as by the power granted the officer by the people of the state — not by personal will, dictate, or desire.

2. When subjects are upset, deescalation techniques can often increase officer safety and lead to positive out-comes, often without the need for the use of force.

Understand that you are not the law; you enforce the law. Peace officers do not make the law; they explain it, enforce it, and encourage others to comply with it. Officers are only legally permitted to do what the law specifically authorizes, not what they want or demand or think should be done when someone becomes verbally abusive.

In this scenario, when asked "why?" Officer Hanson should have said something like this: "I'm asking because the law di-rects any driver stopped by the police to provide their driv-er's license, registration, and insurance. Failure to do so is a violation of the law. I stopped you for speeding. May I please have your license and information?" This reply clarifies that the officer isn't personally requesting these documents; the law demands it. The officer has no personal vested interest, and he is merely doing what the law mandates. That subtle differentiation depersonalizes and deescalates the situation. It's also a very effective way to practice resilience.

I've observed throughout my career that when an officer either makes an interaction personal or takes a subject's reaction personally, or simply doesn't take the time to explain the reason for their actions, subjects often get upset, confrontational, or complain. People may not like what an officer is doing, but if the officer explains that the law requires or authorizes the officer to take certain actions, then at least the person knows it's about what they've done, not who they are. That makes them less likely to resist or argue. I've told suspects, "Hey look, it's nothing personal. You did [whatever the observed violation was], and that violates the law. Now I'm just doing what the law directs me to do. The more you cooperate, the quicker this will be resolved."

All officers are taught deescalation tactics, so remember to use them when someone's upset. Always explain your actions and give the legal justifications. Use the least amount of reasonable force necessary to gain compliance. Fight against the "us against them" or "me against you" mentality. That only fosters or feeds a subject's resistance, defiance, and anger. When you get pulled into that dynamic, it's easy to lose control of your emotions and your reactions. Remain focused on the law, what the law authorizes you to do, while exercising good judgment as to how to most effectively handle the situation.

Another strategy is to focus on the reason for the law. In this scenario, Officer Hanson could explain to the driver that speed is the number one cause of injury collisions, or that traffic enforcement directly correlates to lower traffic deaths and injuries. Usually, when you can calmly, rationally, and impersonally explain all the reasons for your actions, and that the law authorizes your actions, you'll face less resistance.

In addition, in police reports, officers must always legally justify the actions they took. We can never hide, minimize, or misrepresent anything. If we do something wrong, we must be honest about it. We can never lie on a police report, in court, or to a supervisor. To live and serve with integrity, we must maintain the highest level of resilience and wellness.

Therefore, always work under the authority of what the law permits, in the manner that the law authorizes. The law is your shield, not your will, pride, or emotions. That's why it's imperative throughout your career to always be learning. Make sure you know the law inside and out: the penal code, vehicle codes, laws of detention and arrest, laws and techniques of interview and interrogation, case law, and so on. The more of the law you know, the more you will be capable of doing, the more confidence you'll have, and the more successful and safer you will be.

Maintaining Resilience and Motivation

Sometimes, as an officer, it can be hard to maintain our idealism and motivation. It's easy to become burned out from the stress and heartache of the job, especially when there seems to be a lack of support from political leaders and segments of the community, indifferent prosecutors, and an ungrateful public.

When you feel this way, remind yourself that, over the course of your career, you will save hundreds, likely thousands, of people from ever being a victim of crime due to your good police work. There's great nobility and honor in protecting life and serving others. Every time a criminal is put in jail — whether it's for a day or for life — they are unable to victimize others.

Always strive to be the good amidst all the bad. Strive to make a difference with every call, to be useful and helpful to others. Even if you are never thanked, know that your actions will help protect others and even change some people's entire lives. A homeless drug addict might get the help they need because of you. Some people will never forget what you have done for them. Every day will include many opportunities to honorably represent your agency, to support and help your colleagues, and to do good and be useful to others.

A good way to avoid becoming frustrated or demoralized is to focus on only what you can actually control — your integrity, your professionalism and compassion, your attitude, and how you choose to respond to trauma, challenges, and people. Make your goal, at the end of every shift, to be able to say to yourself, "Today I did the very best I could to try to make a difference."

Never forget why you became a peace officer in the first place. Always remind yourself about what you love about this profession and never lose sight of that.

In the video "A Vision of Wellness" (see page 14), Sergeant Ryan Opeka speaks to this well, so I will let him have the last word:

> *Being a cop is something you should be proud of, but it should be part of you, not the whole of you. For me, wellness is having officers that have balance in their life. They're professionals at work, but they're also a person outside of work.*
>
> *So, I've seen a lot of bad things, but I've seen a lot of really cool stuff, too. I've seen teamwork at its best. I've seen people rally together to accomplish a goal.... I've been hugged by victims. I've had families come up and*

just embrace me and thank me for doing the things that I've done for them.

I've seen people save lives, and that's pretty powerful. I've seen someone be resuscitated. I've seen someone who has been written off come back to life. And not just in the medical sense, but I've seen homeless drug addicts turn around and get their life together and by all accounts [they're] living a great life.

I've had suspects that I've arrested, that I've put in jail, come back and thank me for doing that, writing me a thank-you letter saying that, had it not been for me making that arrest, that they don't know where they would be, but they know it wouldn't be in a good place.

I've also seen, while working [during the 2020] riots, families of Black people come up to me and thank me for what I was doing and saying that the things that they were seeing and the forces I was working against and protecting them from, didn't represent their message. I've seen those same people reach out to me and look to make a connection. That gives me a lot of hope that all is not lost and that there's a lot of good people out there that have our backs.

Chapter Two

★

The Nine Warning Signs of Trauma

He who has health, has hope;
and he who has hope, has everything.
— THOMAS CARLYLE

When I put myself through the police academy at twenty-one years old, I had no idea of the kind of evil and heartache I would experience over the next three decades. I eventually learned that the first step toward wellness and resilience is to become aware of the warning signs of trauma. I needed to learn how to recognize the accumulation of daily work traumas and how they affected my behavior, decisions, attitudes, relationships, and health. That way, with self-awareness, I could proactively practice mental, physical, emotional, and spiritual resilience to counteract their potentially crippling effects.

The Nine Warning Signs of Trauma

There are nine basic warning signs that someone is experiencing trauma. If you notice any in yourself, treat them as alerts that you may be falling victim to your profession. These warning signs of trauma don't simply go away on their own. Instead, if not faced and corrected, they tend to progressively and insidiously worsen over time. It's imperative for you and your family members to always be self-aware of any negative changes in your behavior. With increased self-awareness comes the increased capacity to proactively address the issues in constructive ways that restore wellness and enhance resilience.

Any one of these warning signs is a serious indication that someone is having difficulty processing the acute stress and traumas of the job. These warning signs can occur in any combination, and they do not necessarily progress in a certain order. The severity and significance of any particular sign can vary as well. Every person is different.

These are the nine warning signs:

1. Isolation
2. Irritability
3. Difficulty sleeping
4. Anger
5. Emotional numbness, apathy, and disengagement
6. Lack of communication
7. Cynicism, distrust, and dissatisfaction
8. Depression
9. Habitual drinking and other addictive behaviors

All these warning signs present a sharp contrast to the outlook of the idealistic, positive, and enthusiastic officer who graduates from the police academy with high aspirations and a deep desire to protect life and serve others. Any of these symptoms can become crippling unless you practice wellness and resilience *beginning now and daily* throughout your career.

★ "Warning Signs" ★

This six-minute video summarizes the warning signs and symptoms that indicate someone is being significantly affected by daily work traumas, along with addressing the difficulties and stigma of asking for help.

https://www.youtube.com/watch?v=caKDMF2Am2w
Courtesy of LegacyProductions.org

★

---

1. Isolation

Over time there is a natural tendency as a peace officer to become increasingly isolated. This involves withdrawing — preferring primarily the company of work colleagues or being alone rather than associating with other friends and family and joining them in their activities. Officers can develop the tendency to disengage, to not make decisions away from work, and to prefer not to be involved with others — even spouses and children. Eventually, someone can become distant, reclusive, and unapproachable. As someone withdraws, they may tend to think no one understands them and that it's not worth trying to explain anything to anyone. This is an extremely unhealthy way to live or to deal with issues.

Close work bonds are necessary, but we also need the counterbalance of other friends who play a significant role in our overall wellness. Hanging out exclusively with first-responder colleagues tends to reinforce all their negative perceptions and dark views of people. "Outside" friends can help officers maintain a more balanced and positive perspective and can help keep them from developing a victim mentality — that is, feeling victimized by work, the community, and the agency — and also from thinking everyone is a criminal. As someone withdraws in isolation, they tend to become increasingly uncaring, disengaged with life, uninvolved, and disinterested. As this issue intensifies, they can begin to have problems maintaining close, personal relationships and relating with others.

2. Irritability

People coping with trauma often develop a shorter-than-usual fuse, fly off the handle for seemingly insignificant reasons, respond to questions in one- or two-word sentences, usually say they are "fine" just to stop any further conversation, and keep everyone near them walking on eggshells for fear of how they will react. They may seem to be on edge, restless, and always agitated. This occurs with officers because the daily traumas of our profession tend to erode resilience, the ability to cope and to respond to issues in constructive and positive ways.

To help avoid this happening with yourself, it is essential to let your life partner know how important it is for them to tell you how you may be changing as soon as they first notice. It is your job to listen and create an atmosphere where your partner feels comfortable giving you this essential feedback. This will help keep you from unknowingly damaging your relationship. As a peace officer, throughout your career, always remember that your life partner can play a vital role in your emotional survival, resilience, and overall wellness. Both of you need to clearly communicate with each other so you both get what is needed in order to maintain a healthy relationship.

3. Difficulty Sleeping

Having difficulty consistently getting a good night's sleep — either because of sleep interruptions during the night or because someone is only capable of sleeping for a few hours — is a sign that someone is not effectively processing trauma. Good sleep is absolutely essential for the brain to process trauma effectively. As work overburdens the brain, sleep is usually the first thing that goes.

4. Anger

When someone is seriously affected by trauma, they can develop a pattern of taking out their stress and frustration on others, often those they care about most. They will try to create a buffer around themselves, a safe zone where people will just leave them alone. They may use anger to control others, to keep them at a distance, and to avoid taking a real look at themselves and examining what is actually going on inside. They may find themselves enraged and yelling over things that used to never bother them. Acute anger is one of the most corrosive expressions in a relationship.

After a class I was teaching, a Nebraska police officer came up to me with tears in his eyes. He thanked me for the lecture and said softly, "I now realize how terrible I've treated my wife and kids." I took in what he shared, then smiled and told him, "That's great. Now just think of all the things you can do from now on to make it right." He smiled and walked away. We often don't realize all the many ways our job can affect not only us but our life partner and children.

5. Emotional Numbness, Apathy, and Disengagement

For peace officers, becoming emotionally numb is inevitable, at least initially. We need to consistently work to prevent numbness from becoming overwhelming. The job naturally tends to make someone want to shut down emotionally, simply as a way to no longer feel the frustration, stress, pressures, and emotional pain of the job. However, this inevitably leads to seriously damaged relationships at home and an increasing inability to maintain a high quality of life.

6. Lack of Communication

When dealing with trauma, officers often tend to make the mistake of withdrawing and keeping everything inside. Burying and trying to conceal unpleasant emotions and experiences does nothing to help. Those feelings have to come out somehow — if not through expressed communication, then typically through illness, depression, addiction, insomnia, or anger. Reticence to speak also builds on itself. As communication skills diminish, officers may refuse to talk about work at all, and then feelings of depression, anxiety, helplessness, anger, fear, frustration, and other negative emotions can intensify.

7. Cynicism, Distrust, and Dissatisfaction

Another sign or consequence of unaddressed trauma is to become highly dissatisfied at work, extremely cynical, and distrustful of everyone in the world. This cynicism and negative outlook can send someone into a downward spiral that eventually affects every aspect of their life.

8. Depression

Ignoring the warning signs of unaddressed trauma can eventually lead to clinical depression. Left untreated, this may worsen and become potentially severe depression, resulting in substance abuse, broken families and lives, and a host of other debilitating problems, up to and including suicide. Everyone gets depressed from time to time, but address it when it arises. And if it lingers for weeks and months, realize that this can indicate a serious, potentially life-threatening problem.

9. Habitual Drinking and Other Addictive Behaviors

A major warning sign is habitual drinking or compulsively consuming other substances because of a perceived need. About 23 percent of US police officers seriously abuse alcohol, which is about double the rate among the general population. Drinking because of a need or out of habit tends to only intensify problems and emotional issues, making them more serious, and it delays their resolution. If someone is experiencing symptoms of posttraumatic stress injuries (see chapter 6) and they also drink, the chances they will commit suicide increase tenfold. Alcohol consumption is one of the most damaging behaviors for first responders.

At least 20 percent of peace officers will experience at least one serious addiction at some point in their career — whether that's drinking, prescription pills, illegal drugs, gambling, sex, pornography, risk-taking, or any other maladaptive behavior. When our brain becomes injured by the daily traumas of our job, we become prone to develop an addiction. Any compulsive behavior is a major red flag of unreleased and damaging traumas.

Be Self-Aware and Proactive

Maybe the most important component of wellness is self-awareness. If our spirit is suffering from the toxic effects of the job's traumas, we can't do anything, and won't know what to do, if we don't recognize what's happening. In addition, by being self-aware that, as officers, we will struggle, we can prepare for it. We can proactively engage in wellness and resilience practices to prevent the impacts of trauma from accumulating. I have experienced firsthand the tremendous peace and healing that result from practicing the evidence-based wellness strategies I present in this guidebook. These have been shown to significantly enhance overall wellness of the mind, body, emotions, and spirit.

Wellness and resilience start by recognizing the great potential for harm caused by work traumas and the nine warning signs. They also depend upon self-awareness of who you are: of your inner strengths and weaknesses; of how you typically handle stress and difficult emotions; of where you naturally turn for support, healing, and inspiration; and of where you may need to improve or change in order to fortify your spirit and enhance resilience.

Emotional suffering or otherwise being adversely affected by the job of being a peace officer is not a weakness. It is an injury that is inherent in the nature of the work — and these injuries, while they can't always be prevented, can be healed and fixed.

If you have never reflected seriously on the best ways to

mitigate and prepare for the impacts of this work, now is the time. Reflect on this chapter's Self-Awareness Questions and consider how you have dealt with suffering, loss, and pain in the past. Then develop a constructive plan before you need it. Have strategies in place and know what works effectively for you, so you are not caught by surprise or are unprotected when the inevitable challenges occur. There are many ways to respond constructively (which is the focus of chapter 3). Your work is to determine which wellness and resilience strategies resonate with you and then make the conscious effort to practice those daily — with every call and interaction — because every call matters in the long term for your overall wellness.

The peace officer's job is replete with frustrations and sometimes helplessness. We are often unable to save a life, protect a child, catch a perpetrator, or turn a life around. We don't have control over the outcome of our work. All we can control is our own conduct and attitude, by always being professional, consistently doing our job the best we can, and taking care of ourselves and our colleagues. However, if we let them, the job's inevitable failures can start to overwhelm our successes — all those times when we do make a difference in tangible, important ways. One way to recognize when this happens, and to foster self-awareness, is to regularly use the "Coping Guide for Recovery" I provide at the end of this chapter (see pages 36–37).

Our family, loved ones, and life partner can also help us maintain, or regain, self-awareness. It's essential to periodically have detailed conversations with your life partner, at least yearly, to get their perspective on how you're doing. Ask them if you have been changing, if they think the job has been affecting you and the relationship, and how you can help improve your relationship. Don't wait until your partner tells you what my ex-wife said to me: "What happened to you? You're not the person I married. It seems I don't even know you anymore."

Our work as peace officers can be difficult on those who love us. So it's important to periodically acknowledge the difficulties others face because of their love and concern for us, as well as to ask for what we need, in terms of support, from our partner and family. Loved ones don't need or always want to know the details of traumatic events, but they have the absolute right to know whether we're okay. So acknowledge when you've had a disturbing experience that you're trying to work through, and then allow others to support and care for you in the ways they know best.

Self-Awareness Questions

- In your life right now, how do you deal with loss, pain, suffering, and a sense of helplessness? What is most effective?
- What other techniques could you try?
- Do you talk to your life partner or loved ones when you struggle? How can you involve them in your wellness and emotional survival practices?

Case Study: Handling Bad Calls with a Life Partner

Officer Nixon responds to a frantic 911 call of a mother who has just found her two-year-old twin boys unconscious in the swimming pool. Officer Nixon arrives before the paramedics and immediately performs CPR on one child while his partner tries to revive the other. Both children are eventually declared dead, and Officer Nixon consoles the hysterical mother as best he can. He wonders if he'll ever be able to erase her shrieks of tortured anguish from his mind.

When Officer Nixon arrives home that evening, his wife enthusiastically welcomes him home and asks how his day was. Still shaken, not wanting to upset his wife with the horrific details, and not wanting to appear weak, Officer Nixon responds, "I'm fine," and changes the subject. After dinner, he watches television alone in another room. Though his wife senses something is wrong and tries to talk to him several times, he remains distant and noncommunicative all night. His wife is left wondering whether she has done something to upset him. She feels badly about herself, not knowing what to do, and her reaction only makes Officer Nixon feel worse about himself and more determined to hide his emotions better next time.

Case Study Reflection

After a bad call, you may not want to talk about it with others, but never deprive the person closest to you of the crucial information that something disturbing happened. This avoids unintentionally hurting or upsetting someone you love by your reactions to trauma. In this scenario, without going into the details, Officer Nixon could have said something like, "I had a really bad call today. It's too upsetting to talk about, but I'll be okay. I just need some time alone right now."

This way, Officer Nixon tells his wife what he needs, and she won't take his behavior personally. Even better, however, would be if Officer Nixon discusses ahead of time specifically what it means when he says, "I had a really bad call today." Then he and his wife could discuss together what they want and need from each other on those days, and what will be most helpful. In fact, rather than watch television while he's alone,

Officer Nixon would improve his recovery through reflection, so he understands his reactions better. That is the purpose of the "Coping Guide for Recovery" below. Then, at a later time, when Officer Nixon feels ready, he could discuss his reactions with his wife, so she also understands and can help him better in the future.

Coping Guide for Recovery

When traumatic experiences happen, our first impulse can be to want to forget. But it's always more helpful and healing to examine what happened and our reactions in order to understand them better. Use this "Coping Guide for Recovery" as a guide for examining a difficult event, your response, and what you need to heal and recover. You can simply reflect on each item in the list, write out your responses, or discuss these with your life partner, if you feel comfortable doing so.

- *This is what happened:* Express to yourself specifically what occurred.
- *This is how I feel:* Express to yourself all the emotions you are feeling — anger, fear, helplessness, sadness, shame, guilt, depression, and so on.
- *This is what I think about what happened:* Express to yourself all your thoughts about the incident.
- *I recognize that I'm not okay yet:* Acknowledge that you've been hurt, that you're not okay yet. This is perfectly normal and all right.
- *I recognize that I'm safe:* Acknowledge that, in the present moment, you're safe. Take several slow, deep breaths and affirm that in time you will recover.
- *I recognize I don't have to go through this alone:*

Acknowledge all the resources and people available to you. That can include your partner, extended family, friends, colleagues, peer support groups, your agency's employee assistance program (EAP), trauma professionals, therapists, ministers, and so on.

- *This is what I need right now:* Think about your immediate needs and take care of them. This could be food, sleep, exercise, rest, talking to someone, or some type of activity.
- *This is what I can do to recover:* Think about all the helpful and constructive ways you can respond to this trauma in the days ahead. Make a list of actions.
- *I remember to be grateful and to connect with others:* Recall that even though this trauma occurred, you still have good things in your life that you are grateful for. Also make a commitment to connect through positive communication with someone you trust.

Avoiding Compassion Fatigue

Compassion fatigue is when we become indifferent or uncaring and stop wanting to make a difference. This is mainly the result of two things: first, not being steadfast in our own self-care and resilience practice; and second, when we do something hoping for a specific desired outcome and then get discouraged when that outcome doesn't materialize.

Self-care is totally within our control. We must be steadfast in consistently practicing wellness and resilience strategies that fortify, renew, enable, and inspire our spirit — all of which helps keep us motivated to do good.

Discouragement is trickier. As peace officers, we devote our lives to service, and we naturally want our efforts to help others and do good. Many times, we hope for specific positive outcomes, and when those don't result, it's also natural to feel disheartened, disappointed, and frustrated. Eventually, when this happens often enough, we can lose our desire to make an effort, believing no good will come of it and that it's a waste of our time.

The key to avoiding this is to distinguish intentions from outcomes. It's imperative for our overall wellness to strive to be useful and helpful to others, to serve with heart-centered compassion, to believe in our *potential* to do good. But we can never control outcomes. We do good things with the hope these actions will have a lasting, positive influence. The reality is that they may or may not. Ultimately, that doesn't matter. The greatest value, *in the present moment*, is intending to help. That effort will always result in strengthening our resilience. Good intentions always support and improve wellness. They help keep our hearts open and active, which helps us recover from disappointments and traumas. They help keep us inspired and motivated to continue doing good in the future.

Chapter Three

★

Effective Methods to Strengthen Physical, Mental, Spiritual, and Emotional Resilience

It is by going down into the abyss that we recover the treasures of life. Where you stumble, there lies your treasure.
— JOSEPH CAMPBELL

Peace officers are not invincible. At times, our jobs ask us to deal with life's most difficult, traumatic, and even horrific experiences, and then we go home and try to be "normal." But *normal* shouldn't mean ignoring, burying, or pretending we don't feel pain, helplessness, and frustration. Normal means remembering that it's okay to be human and, when we've had a traumatic experience, to take effective steps to cope and heal.

This chapter presents thirty evidence-based resilience strategies you can use to protect yourself, to help work through traumas, and to enhance your physical, mental, spiritual, and emotional wellness. Choose a few that resonate with you and start practicing them *daily* — daily practice is vital to maintain resilience and wellness. Be creative, try different ones, and maintain a proactive approach to strengthening resilience.

Physical Resilience and Fitness
Exercise as a Way of Life

Exercise consistently and refrain from self-destructive behaviors. In my experience, first responders tend to reduce their level of exercise as they progress through their careers. Maintaining a consistent activity level — exercising at least thirty minutes a day, three to four times a week — is essential because it significantly reduces your stress level, reduces your chances of getting injured, and enhances your coping abilities.

Hypervigilance is a major part of our profession, and exercise can reduce tension while you're off duty and enable you to get more consistent sleep, as well as increase your metabolism rate and help prevent weight gain. Consistent aerobic exercise enables you to recover much faster and have renewed energy, and it can reduce by 58 percent your chances of getting a heart attack or acquiring type 2 diabetes. Regular exercise is absolutely vital to your health, mood, and well-being.

La Mesa Police Lieutenant Angela DeSarro shares an experience she had in which exercise changed her life:

After five years spent working patrol, I was selected as a crimes-of-violence detective and was soon working my first murder case. It was a brutal stabbing of a forty-six-year-old drug dealer, who had his throat slit ear to ear. During his autopsy, I noticed out of the corner of my eye, on the next autopsy table, an infant girl being taken out of her small body bag. The infant had passed away from sudden infant death syndrome and appeared to be merely sleeping peacefully, even though I knew different. I remember she had beautiful, soft eyelashes. I kept telling myself not to look at the baby as they cut her chest open to remove her heart and other organs. I couldn't look away. I watched as the forensic examiner used a special electric saw to open her skull and remove her tiny brain. I couldn't help it; I just kept looking and feeling numb.

By the end of the year, I would lose track of the number of cases of senseless violence that I had worked. I had gained twenty-five pounds, was eating poorly, drinking too much, and taking antihistamines in addition to the alcohol in order to sleep. The image of those beautiful, soft eyelashes in my mind just didn't go away. I was depressed, exhausted, and completely consumed with work. I didn't recognize myself in photos. I was feeling weighed down not only by the physical weight gain but also by the incredible heaviness in my chest. I remember trying to get out of bed and feeling the weight in my stomach, and having to roll my body toward the edge of the bed in order to get up. I felt dead inside, like I was just going through the motions. The job I loved so much was slowly drawing the life from my body and spirit.

I'm not sure what the catalyst for change was. I just remember waking up one morning feeling determined to save myself. I think it was the realization that the person I had become was not the person my father had raised. I was a fighter. I needed to find myself again.

I began training for a marathon. In the process of training, I began running half-marathons. I lost the twenty-five pounds I had gained. I felt my physical strength return, the muscles and definition in my body return — it was a complete transformation of my mind, body, and spirit. I was passionate about something again that belonged solely to me.

Running that first marathon was the hardest thing I have ever done. A person's mind can go to very dark places at miles twenty through twenty-six of a marathon. It was the greatest physical and mental challenge of my life, and an even greater spiritual journey. Running changed me. The marathon is a great parallel to life. Being a marathon finisher, I knew there was nothing in life I couldn't accomplish, nothing I could not overcome. Running saved my life.

To date, I have run more than twenty half-marathons and four full marathons. I have offered to help coworkers train for marathons, and I have now trained seven employees, including a sergeant, two dispatchers, three officers, and our chaplain. All of these people had their own reasons for wanting to train. But their reasons for running did not matter as much as the opportunity for self-exploration, growth, and healing. As runners gain stamina and strength, they also build confidence, mental toughness, and an experience that acts as an incredible counterbalance to the trauma and stress of the job.

Eat a Nutritious Diet

Maintain a healthy, nutritious, well-rounded diet. Be extremely careful about alcohol consumption and never drink out of a perceived need. Moderate drinking is defined as one to two drinks, and never more than three, at any given time. As mentioned earlier, first responders who drink are at significant risk to abuse alcohol far more than the general public. First responders who drink and who also have symptoms of post-traumatic stress are ten times more likely to commit suicide.

Do not abuse energy drinks or other caffeinated beverages,

since they dramatically affect the quality of a person's sleep. Consumption of caffeine should stop at least seven hours prior to wanting to sleep, since it takes that long for its effects to wear off. Also, as a society, we are consuming too much processed sugar, such as in sodas, which causes escalating rates of diabetes, weight gain, and heart disease.

Practice Slow, Deep Breathing

"Tactical breathing" is a technique that can be practiced anywhere at any time. It has been shown to immediately reduce stress symptoms, and it can help alleviate certain symptoms of trauma. A calm body is a calm mind, and a calm mind is a calm body. The practice is simple: First, inhale slowly and very deeply through your nose for a count of four. Take as large a breath as you can. Hold your breath for a count of four, and then release all the air through your mouth much more slowly. Repeat this four times.

Mental Resilience and Fitness

Intentionally Choose to Respond Constructively

Set the conscious intention to respond to difficult circumstances in ways that are constructive, helpful, and productive of wellness. See problems as opportunities to choose your character and to learn from. See traumas and setbacks as challenges, not crises. Ask yourself: How can I respond in ways that will affirm my integrity and the good within me. What good can I do now in this situation? What can I do that will enhance resilience?

Remain a Student

Learning involves a search for truth with honesty, humility, and a desire to positively influence others for good purposes. Learning also involves striving to keep our thoughts positive, constructive, and creative. Everything we experience, either bad or good, is first a thought. By learning to keep your thoughts positive, creative, and good, you can unleash your inner power to positively change and affect your circumstances.

As Wayne Dyer has said, "If you believe it will work out, you'll see opportunities. If you believe it won't, you'll see obstacles. Change the way you look at things, and the things you look at will change."

Set Goals

Develop professional and personal goals that are reasonable and attainable. Lay out short-term, intermediate, and long-term goals that you can work toward every day. This will help keep work and life from stagnating. Always have a goal that you are working toward.

La Mesa Police Lieutenant Greg Runge shares his life-plan principle:

It is within our nature to want to improve, to want something better for ourselves in our professional and personal lives, and to feel good about the direction of our lives. I have used a principle I call a life plan, which I reevaluate and adjust every year at New Year's. My life plan for the year is not a simple half-hearted New Year's resolution that is soon broken and forgotten. It is a commitment for the entire year to work on specific physical, mental, financial, and spiritual goals. My objective is not so much to achieve what I had hoped to achieve by the end of the year, but to remain committed to trying every day to do something positive to fulfill my life plan.

I think it's safe to say that we all have in the back of our minds a laundry list of goals, tasks, and intentions that, if they are accomplished, will lift a serious amount of emotional and psychological weight off of our shoulders. This list seems to grow longer the older we get, and year after year, I never seem to get around to crossing anything off. This is true for even the seemingly menial things that I've put off forever while waiting for a couple weeks off so I can tackle them — it seems like that time off never happens.

Sometimes the tasks may relate to physical health, such as losing a specific amount of weight, running a half-marathon, or even getting a medical procedure done. Or the goal can be financial — paying off a credit card, saving a certain amount of money, increasing your retirement fund contributions, or opening an educational savings account for your children.

Some of the biggest tasks can be the hardest to define. These life goals are the very personal intentions that weigh on us year after year and are the most difficult to carry out. Is there a difficult conversation that you've been meaning to have with a friend or family member? An event in your past that has taken an emotional toll that you know you should talk about with someone, maybe even a professional? A broken relationship that you want to repair?

Then there are the mental and spiritual goals, such as studying something new, books you've been wanting to read, or improvements in your character.

Everyone's list will differ. The key to making your own list is to pinpoint the life plan that, if accomplished, will make you feel better about your life. I believe the best chance to make meaningful progress is to choose two or three areas of your life that you want to focus on during the year, and then pick one or two tasks in each area that you will commit to working on each day. Make sure your life plan for the year is reasonable and attainable. Then write it down. A yearly, month-to-month planner is perfect for this. Give yourself sensible goals and deadlines that incrementally push you toward being successful. In your life plan, keep track of where you are, your successes, your setbacks, and hopefully, your ultimate accomplishment — the day you cross the item off your list.

Regarding character improvement and wellness of spirit, it is helpful to list seven to ten character traits or virtues you wish to improve upon. Then, work on one for an entire day, rotate to the next trait or virtue for the next day, and continue through your list one item at a time. When you've finished the list, start again at the beginning, and continue this way throughout the year.

The character virtues may include being more patient, letting go of anger, being more positive, being more helpful to your spouse and others, being more honest, being less negative, not wasting so much time, being more grateful, or any other trait. One of the greatest minds in American history, Benjamin Franklin, wrote a list of thirteen character traits he wanted to work on, and he did so for the rest of his life. His life plan included moderation, justice, sincerity, peace, humility, chastity, cleanliness — in habits, thoughts, and body — industry, silence, temperance, order, being resolute, and frugality.

The objective of this work is to keep yourself on a trajectory of improvement. You may not meet a life-plan goal to your satisfaction at the end of the year, but through consistent effort you will have most assuredly grown closer to reaching that goal.

Discipline Your Will

Train yourself to make better, more-positive, life-affirming choices. Refine your habits, replacing negative or harmful habits with more positive ones. Choose to express yourself in the best way you can. The practice of disciplining the will also involves consistently fulfilling resolutions and objectives, being honest in all things, and living up to all legal, moral, and ethical obligations. Strengthen your conscience by consistently doing what you know is right.

Act with Sincere, Positive Intentions

One of the most meaningful questions we can ask ourselves is why. The reasons we do something — our intentions and motivations — reveal our true character and the quality of our heart. To avoid being controlled by ego and self-centeredness, seek to act with sincere, honest, selfless, and altruistic intentions.

Remember That You Are Not Your Job

You have to work the job; don't be the job. If someone's entire identity is wrapped up in the job of being an officer, then they tend to take every little problem and difficulty on the job very personally. This can cause great bitterness, frustration, and loss of job satisfaction. Realize that being a peace officer is *not* who you are but merely your temporary occupation. The essence of people is never what they do for a living. Rather, we are defined by our character, our actions, and how we affect others' lives. Focus most of your time on that: Develop who you are and nurture your spirit while sustaining deep, personal relationships with the most important individuals in your life. Invest the most in what gives the most lasting value: those activities and relationships that will exist long after you quit working.

Many peace officers have dreamed of pursuing their careers since childhood, and they derive tremendous satisfaction from work. But to maintain that level of satisfaction, and to avoid work becoming a source of significant disappointment, frustration, and despair, you have to remember the distinction between yourself and your job. One day the job will end, and more than most occupations, peace officers are in constant danger of losing their jobs because of injury. For those who view their job as their life, losing their job can feel like the end of their life. Sadly, far too often, this isn't just a figurative end but a literal one as well.

Keep Active

Make keeping active, whether it's spending quality time with loved ones or doing activities alone, one of your highest priorities. Make plans for activities with your partner, children, and friends before you come to the end of your shift and before your days off. Write these plans down, which will help you to follow through on them. Make a conscious effort to show your loved ones that they are the most important part of your day — every day. In addition to wishing they had stayed in better physical shape by being more active, one of the top re-grets of retired first responders is wishing they had spent more time with their children and spouse.

Seek Constructive Solutions

Ideally, being a peace officer should be life-affirming. We are entrusted to protect and enable life and ensure that everyone can live in freedom, security, and peace. Peace officers have the potential to create positive interactions and positive outcomes with every person they meet every day.

Of course, that ideal is rare, and the difficulties of the job can leave officers drained, bitter, angry, frustrated, disengaged, and apathetic. At times, it can be tempting to feel like a victim of problems, people, and circumstances that undermine every effort to do good. To combat this, develop the habit of asking constructive questions. Rather than complaining or feeling like a victim, ask questions like: What can I do to positively change the situation and improve things? Or, how can I keep this from adversely affecting me?

Spiritual Resilience and Fitness
Practice Character-Based Service

Character-based service follows the principles of being self-less, compassionate, useful, and grateful. It involves always learning, being driven to make a meaningful difference, doing as much good as you can, and trying to serve others without self-interest.

One of the most popular classes in the long history of Yale University is "Psychology and the Good Life." This semester-long course examines how to have a peaceful, meaningful, happy life, and the class's evidence-based guidelines will significantly enhance resilience if practiced daily. Here is a summary:

- Practice gratitude always; in everything be thankful.
- Practice positives: think positive, speak positive, have sustained positive beliefs.
- Remain active and engaged with life; especially be active in nature.
- Practice mindfulness, living in the present moment consistently.
- Have a purpose beyond your self-interest, such as striving to compassionately serve and to make a difference.

Serve with Compassion

Search for ways to express and demonstrate heart-centered service with compassion. The virtue of selfless service is fundamental in helping us feel alive and useful. Being useful is one of the greatest human needs other than love.

The most meaningful things in life cannot be seen or touched, but they are felt with the heart. Compassionate service helps you become less self-centered and more useful to others. The more you selflessly give of yourself and try to make a difference and fulfill the needs of others, the more meaning, purpose, joy, and fulfillment you will undoubtedly experience.

A first responder with a vibrant, caring spirit is inspired to solve problems, help those in need, and make the world, their community, and their workplace better. It is important to your spirit to focus on what your partner, children, community, work colleagues, and others need from you rather than what you want from them.

Continually Practice Self-Awareness

Becoming self-aware is an ongoing process. Regularly practice introspection and evaluate how you are doing. How are you changing and growing while on the job? Do you still love your job? How are you sleeping? What more can you do to enhance wellness and resilience? How are your relationships at home, and what can you do to improve them? What can you do to get more out of work? Where can you create positive change and make a helpful difference? Encourage your spouse and family to approach you with any observations or concerns about how you may have changed since becoming a first responder. If they don't approach you, ask them how you have changed, *and listen to the answers.*

Seek Meaning and Purpose

Reflect on what gives meaning and purpose to your life and work. What provides hope, comfort, happiness, and fulfillment? What are your ethics and spiritual values? How do you maintain perspective and keep in touch with the most important people in your life? In what ways do you show the most meaningful people in your life how much you value them?

Who and what are you responsible for, and how consistently do you fulfill that obligation? What purpose do you serve and want out of work and life?

Is your conscience at peace? What can you do proactively to improve yourself, to breathe life into your spirit, and to help yourself feel better about your character and quality of life?

One of the most inspiring books I've ever read is Viktor Frankl's *Man's Search for Meaning*. Frankl survived four years in Nazi concentration camps during World War II, including

Auschwitz. He nearly died several times, and death, starvation, and cruelty beyond description defined every moment for him and his fellow prisoners. He wrote that those few prisoners who survived were the ones who were able to find meaning and purpose by helping others, even while enduring unimaginable suffering daily. The prisoners who gave their daily ration of bread to another starving prisoner, or who tried to comfort prisoners who were dying, were the people who developed a purpose beyond their own mere survival — beyond their own self-interest. This gave them the resilience to survive a place like Auschwitz. Cultivating similar meaningful service can also help you survive a career as a peace officer. Just remember to practice it daily.

Build Your Character

The quality of a person's character is related to his or her integrity, dependability, dedication, trustworthiness, compassion, hard work, and selflessness. The quality of anyone's character can always be improved upon. Strive each day to strengthen yours by consistently choosing to affirm the good in you.

Practice Gratitude

When we remember the truly countless things we have to be thankful for, we naturally avoid dwelling on all those things that could bring down our spirit. To remain positive and deal more effectively with problems, consciously practice gratitude. This will also help keep you connected with the people who mean the most to you, and it will aid in healing relationships.

Be Humble and Open to Learning

Practice humility and understand that there is always more to learn about being a peace officer. The pursuit of excellence depends upon constant improvement and growth. Always strive to learn more about the job, how to be more effective, and how to be more useful to your coworkers, your agency, and your community.

Always be looking for opportunities to learn, and always be passionate about sharing what you know with others. Knowledge and experience are of little value unless shared, and true influence and effectiveness are defined by what we pass on to others. Seek to improve your agency and the level of professional service your agency provides.

The practice of being humble and teachable brings peace and gives a person great strength and the power to lead and influence others. People are naturally drawn to those who are humble, who are sincerely interested in others, always looking to improve themselves and learn, and never concerned with who gets credit or recognition.

Practice Letting Go

Are you aware whenever you dwell on the past or identify with negative thoughts and emotions, and are you able to stop and let go? This is a vital skill for your well-being. Every negative emotion — such as anger, jealousy, envy, hurt feelings, revenge, unforgiveness, and so on — acts as a heavy weight on our spirit and significantly depletes our energy. Every time you become aware of negativity, try to replace those thoughts with more positive ones.

Pay attention to your speech and thoughts and recognize when you are reinforcing negative emotions. But rather than ignoring, reinforcing, or suppressing negative thoughts, learn to acknowledge them and let them go. This will help you develop more positive, constructive patterns of behavior. The book *Letting Go: The Pathway of Surrender* by Dr. David Hawkins is a valuable resource in learning how to let go of all that hinders our well-being. Letting go is a practice that enables us to be fully invested in the present moment.

If you find yourself dwelling on the past or becoming anxious about the future, learn to focus on the present moment. The past can't be changed, so learn to forgive yourself and others — make up for past wrongs as best you can and move forward. As the old saying goes, refusing to forgive someone is like drinking a cup of poison and hoping the other person gets sick.

When you aren't fully invested in the now, within each present moment, then you're robbing yourself of the opportunity to make the present moment both meaningful and productive of wellness.

Embrace the Purpose of Your Profession

There is nobility and honor inherent in the peace officer profession. Our nation and our communities need you to be physically, mentally, emotionally, and spiritually well to provide the essential services of protection.

Before every shift, remind yourself of the purpose of your profession. Never forget the lives you have saved, helped, protected, and positively influenced. And remember that you have the opportunity to make a positive difference in every life you touch.

Practice Your Faith

If you are a person of faith, do not neglect it. Any faith or spiritual practice can be extremely powerful in maintaining a positive, meaningful perspective in life. This has been the single most effective practice in my own life, and it has enabled my spirit to emotionally survive nearly thirty years of acute stress and trauma in law enforcement. Faith can help keep a first responder focused on the true purpose and nobility of the work.

A meaningful faith practice can help keep you from becoming bitter, resentful, self-destructive, or negative, or feeling hopeless and helpless. It provides a powerful counterbalance to and coping mechanism for traumatic work experiences, and it fosters inner peace.

Practice Mindfulness Meditation

I have been practicing meditation for nearly forty years, and I can absolutely say that the best gift you could ever give yourself is to develop the practice of daily meditation. Meditation only involves taking five to ten minutes (preferably in the morning before getting out of bed) to be still, quiet, and at peace while you breathe slowly and deeply. You can quietly focus on one thought that evokes a positive emotion such as gratitude, love, or peace, or maybe think of a problem and ask yourself how you might more effectively deal with it.

Science has shown that meditating for just a few minutes each day has several lasting benefits: It reduces stress and helps to keep you calmer throughout the day; it aids concentration, keeping you more focused and centered; and it enables you to be more at peace.

The San Diego Police Department instituted a mindfulness

meditation practice before officers break from lineup. It has been a very effective way to release the stress that officers may have brought in from home, to center themselves, to become calm and focused, and to prepare for whatever they will face during their shift. If you would like more information on mindfulness meditation for officers, contact the San Diego Police Department (619-531-2000) and ask to speak to their Wellness Unit, which is happy to discuss their program with fellow officers.

Emotional Resilience and Fitness
Value All Relationships

It's important to value all our relationships, not just with those people who are closest to us. Relationships are the foundation for a meaningful, joyful, and fulfilling life — and for a successful career. Be proactive about nurturing and healing all relationships. Never hold grudges, use people, or treat others despairingly. Practice forgiveness, tolerance, empathy, and understanding. Also, consistently act in ways and do things to demonstrate that you value and appreciate others.

I've been a member of the Rotary service organization for several years. They use their relationships within the community and with one another to do a tremendous amount of good through charity and other services. They have a four-pillar test — in the form of four questions we should ask ourselves — that serves as an effective guide for all our interactions with others:

- Is it the truth?
- Is it fair, kind, and compassionate?
- Will it build goodwill and better friendships?
- Is it beneficial to all concerned?

If all our interactions with others consistently follow this guide, then not only will we develop and maintain meaningful relationships, but we will become extremely influential with others.

Maintain Outside Interests

Stay involved with whatever you found fun and interesting *before* becoming a first responder: sports, exercise, hobbies, recreation, coaching, reading, healthy entertainment, travel, volunteer activities, pets, time in nature, and time with children, your partner, and friends outside the profession. Do anything that breathes life into your spirit. After becoming first responders, most people spend significantly more time watching television and using a computer. Such activities tend to keep a person isolated and away from more productive, life-sustaining activities that nurture the spirit and renew their energy.

Join a Cause

Become involved in causes or activities that benefit others. This will help keep you active and involved with persons of similar interests while providing additional meaning to your life. This will help prevent you from becoming isolated and detached, which are among the first signs of becoming adversely affected by the job.

Get Plenty of Sleep

Getting consistently good sleep is vital for emotional wellness. A study by Harvard Medical School found that 40 percent of peace officers have sleeping disorders. In addition, the study showed that, out of five thousand officers, 86 percent slept only four to six hours each night. Seven to eight hours is the recommended amount of sleep that we should get. Lack of good sleep can worsen mood, decrease alertness, interfere with decision-making, impair task performance, cause serious emotional and physical problems, and reduce the ability to concentrate. Eighteen hours of sustained wakefulness, according to the study, is equivalent to a .08 percent blood alcohol level.

Focus Only on What You Can Control

We can't control the outcome of our efforts, and we can't control other people. So focus only on what you have the ability to control: your integrity, how hard you work, your attitude, your reactions to people and circumstances, your compassion, how you choose to respond to people and challenges, and your professionalism. Most stress in life is caused by resisting reality or fighting things we can't change. However, by accepting and making peace with what is beyond our control, we can significantly reduce stress, and the less stress we have, the more capable we are to process trauma. Learn to let go when necessary; otherwise the effort to exert control in all situations can start to control or even cripple you.

Communicate What You're Going Through

It is absolutely crucial to be able to share your experiences, concerns, and issues with someone you trust. All humans are social creatures, and we thrive on engaging with others and sharing information. Peace officers in particular need an outlet for expressing whatever they're going through — which includes processing critical incidents, stress, and trauma, or simply discussing what happened at work that day. Holding in these experiences only increases anxiety, depression, fear, and a sense of isolation. Whether you communicate with a peer, a chaplain, a colleague or friend, a life partner, a trauma professional, a support group, or anyone else, you'll find that continuous, truthful communication is essential to maintain emotional wellness.

Speak and Think Positively

Peace officers can be some of the most negative, cynical, and pessimistic people I have ever known. Given the difficulties of the job, this is understandable, but negativity is a heavy weight that harms our emotional and psychological well-being. It drains our energy, prevents us from responding to challenges and traumas in constructive ways, and reinforces the false belief that we are helpless in any given situation.

So speak and think more positively. Positive thinking doesn't mean ignoring reality or refusing to face difficult problems. Rather, it is a proactive intention to improve our mindset, foster a more constructive attitude, and reframe challenges in positive ways. Instead of feeling negative, victimized, defeated, or helpless, we view problems from a higher perspective and think of constructive ways to manage or mitigate them. When we make a consistent practice of positive thinking, it reduces stress, improves coping skills after trauma, reduces the intensity and duration of depression, awakens our intuition, and improves our overall health.

If you tend to have negative thoughts and a pessimistic or defeatist attitude, develop the habit of thinking and viewing life in more positive and constructive ways. Over time, limiting negative thoughts and letting go of negative emotions will help you sustain a higher quality of life, reduce stress, and maintain your resilience in the face of trauma and challenges.

One of the best ways to do this is to pay attention to what you say. Speech is an outward expression of our thoughts and feelings, so make an effort to say only what is true, helpful, encouraging, and positive. You may find this increases your influence and impact. A positive mind anticipates happiness, joy, health, success, improved opportunities, and favorable results. With a positive attitude you can experience greater hope and more pleasant feelings, and you can visualize the results you want to achieve.

Maintain Your Life-Work Balance

It's essential to maintain a healthy life-work balance; therefore refrain from working too much overtime. You should love your job, but you should love your life a whole lot more. Keep your personal life separate from the job and don't neglect it. Your personal life does not just take care of itself. If left unattended, it will deteriorate. Whether you love camping, hiking, biking, being in nature, volunteering, coaching, gardening — do something as an outlet to take your mind away from the job.

Take responsibility for maintaining, nurturing, and enjoying your personal life. Your personal life is, in fact, your "real" life, and your job as a peace officer should be only a complementary part of it. If you find that you passively allow work stress and the demands of the job to impose on or take over your personal time, make a conscious effort to restore a healthy balance. Work to live, don't live to work. During personal time, you can breathe life into your spirit, enjoy your relationships, and enhance your overall wellness.

───── ★ "Wellness Strategies" ★ ─────

The three-minute video "Wellness Strategies" discusses a range of everyday wellness and resilience strategies, and it includes descriptions of CopLine (see Resources) and the San Diego Police Department's Wellness Unit.

https://www.youtube.com/watch?v=sU_N-8vCdCg
Courtesy of LegacyProductions.org

──────── ★ ────────

Self-Awareness Questions

- In what ways do you currently release or manage stress?
- How effective and healthy are these outlets?
- Can you improve them?
- What else can you do daily to enhance your mental, physical, emotional, and spiritual well-being?

Case Study: Solving the Larger Problem

For the third time in the same shift, Officer Sara Chan receives a call to respond to a homeless transient causing problems outside a business downtown. Over the last few years, these types of calls have increased dramatically, and she and the other officers have grown tired of dealing with the homeless, many of whom have mental health issues. The officers see the same people day after day causing the same problems.

When Officer Chan arrives, she already feels very frustrated and angry. The disruptive transient, a man she's dealt with before, is yelling incoherently at passersby. Officer Chan gets in his face and yells at him to move on, telling him to stop coming back. After a while, the man shuffles away, but Officer Chan knows she hasn't fixed anything. It's just a matter of time before she gets another call.

Case Study Reflection

Because of her frustrations, Officer Chan treats this call like a nuisance and simply chases the transient away. This solves the immediate problem, but it does nothing to help fix the ongoing quality-of-life issue for local residents and businesses, and it does nothing to help the person living on the street. Instead, she should put aside her own anger and try to come up with more creative ways to solve the larger problem so she doesn't have to keep coming back.

Perhaps the most effective and compassionate choice would be to help the homeless man get the resources and assistance he needs. To determine his particular needs and situation, she could talk with him. She might find out why he keeps coming to this particular street or business and whether he has any family or other resources he might go to or contact instead. She could investigate what agencies help people with his particular problems and put them in touch. That might involve contacting the local court system and prosecutors or local nongovernment agencies and nonprofits. She could also talk to the local businesses and determine whether they are doing anything to encourage transients to panhandle or loiter in the area.

On her own, Officer Chan might not be able to solve the larger problem, but by recognizing it and doing what she can to coordinate resources and get everyone involved, she might uncover a constructive solution. In this scenario, Officer Chan responds to her own frustrations by moving the transient along, but this simply passes the problem along. If she responds instead with a sense of purpose to fix the overall situation, her efforts might benefit everyone: the transient, the businesses, the residents, and herself.

Peer Support: Taking Care of One Another

Peer support is another essential aspect of wellness and resilience. Don't use the strategies presented in this chapter just to benefit yourself. Keep an eye on your brothers and sisters in law enforcement, along with anyone you serve with, and help them to maintain wellness and to cope with and recover from traumas. I know of three officers from my agency who would have committed suicide were it not for the compassionate and caring actions of their colleagues. Whether you are on your agency's peer support team or not, every peace officer has the fundamental and ethical responsibility to proactively support their colleagues.

We need to care about *everyone* we work with — not only because it's the right thing to do, but because our own safety, survival, and well-being depend upon their wellness and resilience. Take a personal interest in your colleagues and be concerned for their well-being. Look for the warning signs of trauma and, as soon as you recognize them, reach out. If someone seems upset or their behavior changes, say something like, "I notice you haven't been yourself lately. Are you all right? Let's get a cup of coffee and talk." Or, "That was a really bad call.

How are you doing?" When the officer inevitably responds, "I'm fine," don't let it go. In whatever way is appropriate, keep asking and checking in until they give an honest answer or you are sure they really are fine.

As a profession, we haven't yet reached the point where officers feel that, not only is it okay to ask for help, but it's okay to notice that a colleague needs help and to offer support in meaningful ways. Yet we need to get to that point, so that this is both universally accepted and even *expected*. Every peace officer will need help — and be needed to help other officers — many times throughout their career.

Make sure to review this book's Resources section. This includes a range of agencies, websites, and books that provide advice and offer direct support to help you and other first responders recover from the traumas inherent in our profession.

It takes courage to tell someone, "Something's going on inside I don't like. I might need some help." Every peace officer could use understanding and support. When necessary, do your part to get the help you need as well as to help your colleagues get the help they need.

Chapter Four

★

Survival Lessons

Live as if you were to die tomorrow.
Learn as if you were to live forever.
— MOHANDAS GANDHI

We can learn invaluable survival lessons from our peace officer colleagues. Our colleagues have experienced the same struggles, frustrations, debilitating stress, traumas, critical incidents, and sense of helplessness we have, or that we all will one day. An integral aspect of wellness training is learning from the experiences — both good and bad — of others and then integrating those survival lessons into our own daily personal wellness practices. That is the focus of this chapter.

San Diego Police Department: A Wellness and Resilience Study

During 2011 a number of troubling incidents plagued the San Diego Police Department (SDPD), where in less than a year they had two officers murdered, one committed suicide, two died in accidents while off duty, and nearly a dozen faced legal charges for everything from fixing tickets to sexual assault. This prompted an extensive study of the department that attempted to pinpoint the causes of acute stress and discord among the officers and the effects of trauma. Information from this study and research into the wellness practices of other agencies led to the establishment, also in 2011, of the San Diego Police Department's Wellness Unit, which in 2016 won national recognition from the National Law Enforcement Officers Memorial Fund for their proactive wellness initiatives.

The SDPD study was led by Julia Holladay, a researcher for the University of San Diego, and it included personal interviews with SDPD officers. From these firsthand accounts, researchers extrapolated the most helpful, practical methods for recovery and survival. What follows are the most important and most-often-cited concerns and lessons the study identified, along with quotes from the officers who participated in the study. Ultimately, the study highlighted issues typical of any peace officer agency, and the study participants described experiences common to all peace officers.

The Struggle against Hypervigilance

I do try to leave work at work, but I didn't think trauma was affecting me in my home life. I don't want to lose control. I go to houses to help others cope, and I'm losing control of my own home.

The insidious nature of the peace officer's job is that it fosters hypervigilance. The damage is like a slow, malignant cancer growing in our consciousness and spirit. Before we realize it, we can become overbearing and obsessive about controlling people. We tend to become suspicious of everyone and treat our spouse and family like criminals.

A peace officer often avoids "losing control" of their home by making every effort to remain engaged in the activities and interests of their family. Yet officers don't deserve to be treated any differently because of their job. Your family needs you and deserves to have you physically, mentally, emotionally, and spiritually present and engaged with them consistently, without trying to control them or telling them what to do.

You always look for people with an ulterior motive. You eventually don't trust anyone anymore, and you always look at the "what if." You become extremely cynical. I am aware of so many things that people do — things that it would be better not to know. It's hard to turn that knowledge off.

It's important to remember that being an officer is a job; it is not who you are. The love we experience with our families and friends away from work, as well as our active pursuits outside of work, are what breathes life into our spirits. Most people are basically good and have good intentions. Statistics show that only about 2 percent of people are criminals. It's just that officers deal with those 2 percent nearly 100 percent of the time, so their view of people and the world can become very skewed if they're not careful. Not everyone is a criminal.

It's also important to remember that there is more to a peace officer's job than putting people in jail. I always loved putting people in jail and even did so as a captain because, when in jail, criminals weren't molesting, robbing, or killing others. But by far the most fulfilling moments I had in my career were those times when I was able to do something extra to help someone, to solve a problem, and to make a meaningful difference in someone's life.

Here at work, you need a command presence and hyper-vigilance. On patrol or taking a radio call, you have to make split-second decisions, so you are ramped up and expedient. When you go home you are still in it, mentally and physically, and you have to make that shift. If you don't catch yourself, you begin making quick decisions and people at home don't want you to fix it. They may just want you to listen.

This is an extremely important point. As peace officers, we are expected to solve everyone's problems quickly, to be assertive and take care of business. However, this doesn't work in our personal relationships. Our spouse and children do not want us to solve all their problems. They mainly want and need us to listen, to offer emotional support, and to be there for them in the way they want and need, not to respond in the way we would on the job. When our life partner is sharing something with us or speaking of a problem, they mainly just want to connect with us and to be heard and validated.

At times it can be challenging to exercise patience and to calmly listen with understanding and caring to everyday problems that seem much less serious than the problems we encounter on the job, such as pursuing armed robbers or helping survivors of a car crash. If a life partner complains about a co-worker or boss, or expresses frustration with the children, an officer might think, *What's the big deal? Are you serious?* If you feel the urge to dismiss the problems of a loved one, remind yourself that their issues, problems, and concerns are just as important to them as yours are to you, and resist displaying impatience in your body language.

The stress comes home with me. But you have to learn how to shut it off. Off duty you are always on, and the stress can kill you.

Maintaining emotional balance and keeping the proper perspective is essential to maintaining the wellness of your spirit. As one officer said: "You have to realize the damage this job has the potential of doing and cultivate the ability to adjust to it to stay healthy by working on resiliency every day."

The Urge to Shut Down and Disengage

I used to come home and shut down. I would come home and feel like a zombie, just wanting to sit and watch TV and not do anything else. Now I try and take a lot of time off. I like to spend it with my kids, but it's harder to make it work with my wife.

Before, in the first year on the job, I was really shut off. I was engaged that year, and my fiancée told me how she felt like she was walking on eggshells around me. I don't want someone to feel that way around me, so it was definitely good feedback. If you don't know the problem, it's hard to fix. It wasn't hard to open up once I did. I just didn't want to expose others to my issues, but then I thought, "Hey, if they are opening up to me, it's not fair not to open up myself."

Problems start when you let things get out of hand, like drinking too much or being promiscuous. Some guys keep things bottled up and then blow up. They don't include their wife or family in things. When I talk to my wife, she is totally aware of what's going on, whereas a lot of my friends have wives who are totally clueless. Keeping it in internally and not including family makes it hard.

Any peace officer who wonders whether they have changed since starting their job or whether the job has negatively affected them need only ask their life partner, a family member, or a close friend. Typically, changes in behavior occur quickly and are dramatic. Life partners often say they no longer understand their first-responder mates, and they don't like the person their mates have become. They describe their mates as shutting down immediately upon coming home. Their mates don't talk or share anything about work, and they tend to be always tired, moody, and disengaged and want to be left alone. Partners can rarely get their mates to participate in making family decisions, even something as simple as where to go out to eat. First responders may use a favorite chair like a baby uses a pacifier. Spouses don't know what they can talk about with their first-responder mates, when to bring up issues or problems, or how to get their attention in general. Life partners also complain that their partners rarely want to do anything fun or spend time with neighbors and friends outside the peace officer profession. Close friends or other family may notice that the officer has become increasingly judgmental, critical, negative, and distant.

All these comments are typical. Serious relationship and emotional problems can arise if work stress and traumas aren't addressed and if officers fail to maintain a healthy work-life balance. It is true that spouses can never fully understand what an officer experiences at work — and this is probably a good thing. However, there is a middle ground between saying nothing and telling everything. When your life partner asks about your day, they don't necessarily want to hear every detail of the child molestation case or what the mangled bodies in an accident looked like. They might want some details, but what they really want and need to know is *how you are doing*. They want to know that you are all right and to understand generally how the day affected you and if there is anything they can do to help.

As I've said, when you have had a particularly disturbing day, let the people closest to you know that, even if you don't want to discuss the details. Tell others specifically what they can do to support you. Your life partner, family, and close friends are your greatest source of support, comfort, and peace, so don't shut down around them or push them away! Foster your connections with those you love, and in return, they will typically do anything in their power for you.

Also, make time for your family and friends away from work. Many times, officers retire with hundreds of hours of vacation still on the books. This is such a waste. Periodically use your time off to replenish your spirit and to spend meaningful time with your family. If you want your family to be your greatest support, then consistently find ways to be engaged and involved with them. Be a communicative, attentive partner who cares the most about the ones you love the most.

> *I believe in the book* Emotional Survival for Law Enforcement *[by Kevin Gilmartin] and see a lot of myself and other officers in that book. It should be part of the curriculum in the academy and tested on, because it could save careers and marriages. In fact, the whole family should read it.*

Books can be a vital resource not only for peace officers but for their partners and families. They can help a spouse understand what a first responder's life is like and how best to support and care for them. In the Resources, I provide a list of recommended books, which includes *Emotional Survival* by Gilmartin and *I Love a Cop* by Ellen Kirschman. My previous wellness and resilience guide, *Bulletproof Spirit*, is required reading at the FBI National Academy and other academies throughout America.

The Constant Danger of Stress, Depression, and Isolation

If you're alive, you've survived. The adrenaline has its highs and lows with hypervigilance, and part of the balance is having an outlet away from work and people to talk to. A physical outlet will help to some degree, but you need an emotional outlet, too.

I feel like I want to be a hermit. I am usually someone who likes to be out doing something, biking, hiking, walking my dog. I still function, but when I feel this way, I am not in the happy place of feeling normal — my normal.

Police work has higher stress than most jobs, and the stress builds unless you remain active. If I don't go run and instead stay home like a couch potato, I don't have an outlet for my stress.

Officers often express how hard it can be to fend off stress and depression. Winding down from hypervigilance can undermine their intention to be active, creating a negative cycle in which they give up on making the effort. Before not doing things becomes a habit, make plans for your days off, write those plans down (which makes you more likely to follow through), and then follow through.

Workplace Gossip and Officer Morale

It is emotionally and mentally painful to be on the end of the gossip chain.

In a nutshell, I can deal with people outside this division, the citizens and the criminals; it was the people under this roof that I couldn't deal with — bad-mouthing me and getting in the way of my career.

Officers in the study spoke about how gossip, derision, and malicious rumors can have devastating effects on the morale of individuals as well as on the agency as a whole. Actively spreading rumors is one of the worst things peace officers can do to one another. It sabotages the wellness and resilience of one of their own and becomes a reckless cancer within an agency. People should be called out when they do this or perpetuate it, since it harms the very people they depend on for their own protection, for their very lives. Stand up when you hear gossip, saying something like, "That's not helpful."

As one police officer put it: "We can take a life in a moment's notice, so we have to have trust, to look after each other, and do it honorably in ways that are supportive."

The Difficulty of Asking for Help

I am supposed to know how to help others. I don't want to be "that guy" with the dysfunction. I guess I haven't felt I've needed to ask, and I didn't want to be one of "them."

Peace officer culture places a high value on appearing strong and self-sufficient, and it tends to stigmatize anyone who asks for help. Unfortunately, this leads officers to want to handle problems privately. However, as one officer in the study stated: "You have to understand you are not going to be weak if you ask for help. A peer-support team member was my mentor. He didn't sugarcoat stuff and actually cared. Being humble has a lot to do with it."

Suffering in silence kills more peace officers than anything else. The effects of trauma just don't disappear over time; if not faced, they're likely to significantly worsen. We cannot outlast trauma or will it way. We can't ignore it or pretend it doesn't exist.

As the officer noted, it takes humility to ask for help. Humility is one of the greatest character virtues, and it's essential to help maintain wellness and resilience. Officers are not superheroes; they are human like everyone else. They're just as vulnerable and just as susceptible (if not more so) to pain, suffering, and emotional trauma because of what they experience daily.

If an officer's leg were seriously injured during an altercation, they would go to the doctor. Why aren't mental, emotional, and spiritual injuries treated the same way, by seeking professional help? Emotional trauma isn't weakness; it's an injury that impacts someone's ability to function and effectively do their job.

If someone stubbornly (and stupidly) refuses to get help when they need it, they are in fact making themselves weaker and more susceptible to further injury. It takes courage to seek help, but that assistance is necessary to fully recover from trauma. Only then can we be the best we can be for others — not only for our family and our colleagues but for the thousands of people in our community who depend on us for their safety and even survival.

> *You are supposed to be the one helping and not asking for help. From what I've heard from others in the past, those who needed help were looked at negatively. Today, there seems to be less of a stigma because I've heard officers talk about the help that is available. I went for help after a shooting because I was second-guessing what I could have done differently. Counseling was incredible because I got to debrief full-on, talking about the entire incident from beginning to end with my wife sitting there, which made her understand everything.*

> *Often officers internalize and think to themselves: "I'm tough. I have no weaknesses. I can take care of myself." Because officers who survive the job learn how to identify what's wrong, they can then seek help and find the tools to make things better.*

As these officers expressed, attitudes about seeking help are slowly changing, but there is a long way to go. More and more, officers are recognizing that it's okay to be human, that being well mentally and emotionally is a good thing, and that part of being tough — and smart — is being self-aware and honestly evaluating what we need, and then being strong enough to seek assistance. We all need help sometimes, *especially as a peace officer.* As a profession, we need to reach the point where it's not just all right to seek help, but it is *expected* that at times during every peace officer's career they are going to need help.

We don't want to be seen as weak amongst our peers and that's the stigma. If you want and need to get help, your ego says, "No, you don't need help." You have to get outside that voice, rise above it, and if you really need it — get the help. We want to be seen as strong and self-sufficient, and we guard our privacy.

For someone I am close to in the department, I would suggest getting help: go do it. For myself, I would get help if I needed it, but wouldn't tell anyone. There are resources available, but when is the culture actually going to change?

Maintaining privacy is an important issue. Clearly, as these officers expressed, the fear of being seen to need help can keep officers from getting help. Tens of thousands of first responders are needlessly suffering from posttraumatic stress, acute stress, and depression because they choose not to get the evidence-based help that can restore and heal them. However, it's always possible to get help for trauma while also maintaining privacy. Legally, and as a matter of department policy, all help officers receive is kept strictly confidential. But this fear will likely continue to keep officers from doing the right thing until the stigma around seeking help goes away.

I needed to go to the counseling service. I made an appointment and the trauma professional gave me a test to see how depressed I was. Out of a score between one and ten, I got an eight, which is high. I didn't even know I was depressed, and that's scary. It goes to lack of awareness, not as much about stigma.

Those who don't get help get depressed and then begin not to care, so they drink, gamble, use drugs, and go down the cesspool that can lead to suicide — all because they won't get help.

Officers who don't have access to resources get so stressed and backed into a corner — yeah, that's scary. Maybe that's why suicide rates are so high among officers? There is a correlation between the two. When officers get into trouble..., they were probably not seeing someone for help. Sure, others may notice signs, but the person wasn't seeking help.

I went to the counseling services for work trauma and a resulting drinking problem; that was the hardest thing I ever did. I would get home from work at 4 p.m. and be at the bar by 4:10. How I made it home without being pulled over I will never know.

The officer above undoubtedly saved his career by being aware and smart and getting help when nothing else was working. Drinking, substance abuse, promiscuity, depression, gambling, and psychological and emotional distress are symptoms of an underlying cause — typically acute stress or trauma — that has not been effectively processed in a healthy manner.

As all of these quotes make clear, the tough persona of peace officers is often what makes it so difficult for these same officers to ask for help, even when they know they need it. To protect this persona, it's almost as if officers are willing to lose their career, their spouse, and everything they love. However, the pride in this image and the stigma of seeking help have resulted in the senseless deaths of more officers from suicide than from all assaults, killings, and accidents combined. Every year, suicide is the leading cause of death among officers. Real warriors do what is needed in order to be well — in mind, body, and spirit — so they can take care of those who need and love them.

The Importance of Peer Support

The stigma is that you are not in control and there must be something wrong with you. Peer support [by] officers on critical incidents helps because you are hearing from a fellow cop who understands that if you get a full plate, it is okay to ask for or seek other help. This stigma is hard to overcome because cops feel like they have to handle anything that comes their way. The department fosters independent thought. Having the wellness unit and other viable resources with peers to talk to or people with experience is helpful. The job can have a negative effect, and if you don't have support, it can get to a boiling point and affect you professionally and personally.

I think if an officer is approached by a supervisor, mentor, or someone who is genuinely interested in their well-being, he may be more likely to get necessary help than if left to his own devices.

The fastest way to end the stigma over seeking help is for supervisors and officers to take a personal interest in the wellness of those they work with and depend upon. It's imperative for supervisors and managers to be leaders in this regard and make the mental and emotional well-being of their officers a priority.

Peace officers must pay attention to each other and actively look for ways to show concern and to take better care of one another. Compassionately showing genuine concern for fellow officers and dispatchers could significantly help others deal with whatever issues they may have. It could save a career — or a life.

Talking with peers who have experienced similar things is often the very thing necessary for understanding and healing to occur. That is why a peer-support team is essential, even critical, for every peace officer agency. All officers share similar trauma experiences, and therefore they can understand what their colleagues are going through like few others. Officers are uniquely united in this, placing them in the best position to provide understanding and support for one another.

I had one officer tell me he was going to bill me for all the help he was giving me through my divorce. He is just a buddy, a really good guy. He used to text me and call me to check up on me and would say, "Let's meet for lunch." He reached out to me, and I didn't have to ask him. I am the type who won't ask for help unless I am offered. When I know I need it, I'll take it.

This is a great example of how peace officers can look out for and help each other. What a great way to assist a coworker going through a tough time. First responders need to always remember that their survival depends on the wellness and resilience of their brothers and sisters working beside them. Maintaining our colleagues' well-being is in our best interests. We all depend on each other to go home safe every night, and wellness (coupled with good training) is the cornerstone of officer safety.

On Being a Person, Not a Job

As the following officers make clear, the peace officer profession can tend to overtake your life. It's essential for you to cultivate friendships, interests, and activities outside of work. These meaningful interests and activities will be there long after your career has ended.

I think that some officers take their job too seriously. What I mean by that is that the job is their life. They do not have anything else outside the department. Officers need non-work-related outlets; otherwise it will eat them alive. Also, I don't think people actually grasp what they are getting into when they start this job.

The job is what I do, not who I am, because in the beginning I would think, "I'm a cop.... I'm a cop." I am not that way anymore. I am still proud of what I do, but it isn't everything anymore.

I have pictures of my kids in my office for a reason: They are plastered on my wall to remind me why I am doing this and who depends upon me. Outside interests are huge. Officers say they have friends who are not cops, but it is scary how many really don't. They can't admit it to themselves. I know an officer friend who retired a few years ago, and he is lost because all of his friends were officers and they work.

I have close friends who are not PD because it gives me a big reality check. Not everyone is a dirtbag, a suspect out to get you, and there is kindness in the world. It keeps me grounded not to be with police department people. I have friends who are close enough to me to tell me that, "No, you are not rolling down my window so you can yell at that guy," or "Stop eyeing someone who looks suspicious," or "Stop being a cop for more than five seconds."

There have to be roles that are more important than being a cop. There are roles like wife, mother, husband, father, coach, or youth leader, something more important because the job doesn't last forever.

In terms of surviving emotionally, you have to have strong social bonds, loving and caring relationships, and a solid support group. Without support, you'll fall. I also have friends outside the department. I see that some officers who retire die soon after because they don't have other interests and their whole life has been about being a cop, and that's all they know. I've always had something, other interests.

The Importance of Resilience

Self-awareness is key, and a good officer has this. I sometimes observe officers and think to myself, "He's never going to retire." You see what mistakes they are making and can just tell that they will do something to sabotage it. There were over eighty people in my police academy, and there are only eleven of us left.

Trainees see me as easygoing and talk to me. I try and tell some that this job isn't for everybody and there is no shame in deciding you don't want to deal with this. Bad outcomes are many: domestic violence, alcoholism, suicide. The stuff that goes into this job takes its toll. It's hard because we can't control everything. Successful officers know that there are some things that just can't be controlled no matter how hard we try. You have to learn to let go.

The bottom line is you have to care about people. It's not all about putting people in jail.

As this extensive university study for the San Diego Police Department demonstrates, officers need to focus on their physical, spiritual, mental, and emotional resilience and wellness. We can learn invaluable lessons from those who work by our sides and who themselves have struggled to find ways to recover from trauma and to maintain optimal wellness.

★ "Code 9: Officer Needs Assistance" ★

This eight-minute video includes several police officers, trauma professionals, and loved ones discussing the personal effects of trauma among officers. It includes reflections on several officers who committed suicide.

https://www.youtube.com/watch?v=SJ_-qHhvaug
Courtesy of "Code 9 — Officer Needs Assistance"

★

Maintaining Personal Relationships and Seeking Help

An officer's job is constantly challenging. The nature of dealing with daily work traumas can tend to suffocate someone's heart — making effective communication, connecting and relating to others, and caring for oneself more difficult to sustain.

The first line of support is to maintain your personal relationships. In particular, protect the relationships that are most important to you, the ones you derive the most from. Never take these relationships for granted. Instead, actively cultivate and improve them by being caring and helpful to these people, knowing that they may one day be your lifeline, offering meaningful support when you need it most.

An officer from Southern California shared with me that one way his job has changed him is that he now must make a conscious effort to be nice to his seven-year-old son. He said, "I have to keep reminding myself that he's not a little crook; he's my boy. Be nice to him. Spend some time with him and play with him. I have to make myself do that. It doesn't come natural to me anymore." Remember this officer, and actively do whatever you can to show your loved ones *each day* that they are the most important people in your life.

Then recognize and overcome any internal resistance you have to seeking help. As the officers in the SDPD study described, this might include fear of the stigma that other officers may think you're weak or that something's wrong with you; fear of what your spouse or friends may think; fears about confidentiality; personal bravado or thinking you're too tough to ever need help; believing the effects of trauma will just go away over time on their own; or thinking that you're all alone — that no one else has experienced what you are experiencing. *All* of these barriers are self-imposed. They are only real if you make them real in your own mind. There is never *any reason* why someone shouldn't get help when they are in pain or struggling to cope.

It's important to remember that it is literally impossible for you to feel something that *every other* peace officer hasn't also felt at one time or another. Not every officer will admit this, and some hide the magnitude of the traumas they have experienced, but those who do are hurting themselves, and indirectly hurting their loved ones.

Often, a seemingly insignificant incident can unleash a torrent of disturbing thoughts and emotions. That's the nature of trauma and how it accumulates. You can never know when the brain has just had enough and will begin to not function normally — that's the sign of serious injury. But these injuries can be healed with a complete recovery and restoration of a normal life.

You absolutely are not alone. There are about 900,000 peace officers currently employed in America, and over 120,000 of them suffer from severe posttraumatic stress, and hundreds of thousands more suffer from sleep disorders, depression, anxiety, intrusive thoughts, uncontrollable emotions, mental and emotional distress, and all the other symptoms of trauma. *A human being is incapable of being a peace officer and not in some way be impacted by trauma.* This means every officer will need some help at some point, or even at many points. That's perfectly normal and needs to be accepted.

I've trained over seven thousand peace officers in North America, and I always ask the same question: "Are you the same person you were when you got hired?" I have yet to have any peace officer, whether they were in FTO training or were a longtime veteran, tell me that the job had not adversely affected them in a myriad of ways. Be a warrior of spirit and take control of your wellness. Protect your relationships with loved ones and reach out for help when you need it.

Self-Awareness Questions

- What are your most important personal relationships, and what makes them important?
- In what ways can you improve your relationships and your overall relatedness to people?
- Would you ever confide to a peer or seek help if you thought you needed it or if your spouse told you that you needed to? Why or why not?

Case Study: Supporting Peers

Six detectives at one agency have a routine of all going to lunch together every day. Without ever saying why, one male detective starts disappearing at lunchtime and going off on his own.

Then one day after returning from lunch, the other five detectives notice that the one detective is sitting in his car crying. No one approaches him or says anything, and this goes on for several weeks.

However, behind the lone detective's back, his fellow investigators laugh at him and wonder what is wrong with the guy. But no one is ever brave enough to walk over and ask.

Case Study Reflection

This situation really happened and was told to me by one of the detectives involved. He never shared what happened to the distressed detective, but he felt great remorse for not reaching out to him. What was obvious to that detective was that they let their colleague down. One of them should have approached him in a caring way and tried to help. If you notice a fellow officer hasn't been themselves lately, reach out. Let them know they aren't alone.

It is my belief that peace officers who commit suicide often do so because they think no one cares about them. If no one cared enough to even notice that they were troubled, then why would anyone care if they were gone? This kind of thing wouldn't happen if, in our profession, it was accepted and normal to notice when a colleague needs help and to reach out to support them.

In the situation above, there is no way that the lone detective would have been able to practice officer safety when he was so troubled — that imperiled the safety of the entire team. Peer support is exactly what that says. It means *supporting our peers* so that they — and we — can be safe and well.

Resilience Means Doing What You Can

When we are in a tough place, when our heart aches constantly and everything seems bad, it can be hard to know what to do to feel better and be resilient.

But resilience is strengthened each time we reframe our challenges so that we don't view ourselves or our situation as hopeless. Resilience is strengthened each time we affirm the good in ourselves; each time we try to help, be useful, and make a meaningful difference; each time we intentionally choose to do good and act with integrity during a bad situation; each time we intentionally practice a wellness strategy.

To keep from feeling defeatist, search for what good you can do within the present moment, rather than focusing on a sense of helplessness. Even the smallest gestures of empathy or kindness to a suffering victim can offer great hope and soothe some of their pain. Focus on remaining professional, compassionate, and helpful in positive ways no matter what is before you. You have the absolute power and control to do that. Choosing to do what you can will strengthen resilience and foster wellness every time.

Chapter Five

---★---

The Spiritual Resilience of Service

I serve to be of some use for the greater good of others.
I no longer live for what I want, but in how I can serve by
keeping others in the sanctuary of my heart.

— ANONYMOUS

When the practice of spiritual resilience is both compassionate and life-affirming, then our actions will be productive of wellness for more people than just ourselves. No story illustrates that better than this:

In 2017, during an early September morning in Albuquerque, New Mexico, police officer Ryan Holets responded to a radio call about a petty theft that had just occurred in a convenience store. Most officers would have handled this routine call in a few minutes and moved on to do something else less mundane, but Ryan was always looking to make a difference.

As Ryan left the store, he noticed a couple sitting on the grass against the building. Both were in the act of shooting heroin into their arms. As he approached, Ryan saw that the woman was about eight months pregnant.

Thirty-five-year-old Crystal Champ looked up at Officer Holets with sunken, ghostly eyes that couldn't conceal years of addiction and hopelessness. Ryan told her to stop, that she was going to kill her baby. Crystal just lowered her head and began crying. Through her tears she told Officer Holets that she knew she was a horrible person but that she had been homeless and addicted to heroin and methamphetamine for over fifteen years. She said the drugs controlled her life and that she had to do heroin to keep from getting sick. As she explained later, "I did give up. I just decided this was going to be my life."

Crystal told Officer Holets that she desperately hoped that maybe someone would adopt her baby and give her a chance at life. In that moment, Ryan no longer saw a worthless, homeless drug addict but a desperate mother, a suffering woman who had lost all hope. Ryan was always trying to make a difference in his service as an officer. He says, "I'd gotten tired of seeing so many situations where I want to help but can't. And in that moment, I realized that I had a chance to help."

Officer Holets opened his wallet and showed Crystal a photo of his wife and four children, including a ten-month-old baby, and he offered to adopt her baby. Then Ryan drove in his police car to meet his wife, tell her what he had just experienced, and ask if they could adopt the baby. His wife, knowing her husband's heart, agreed immediately.

Hope Holets was born three weeks later. Afterward, Ryan and his wife gave Crystal the opportunity to say a final goodbye to her newborn daughter. Crying tears of hope and gratitude, her eyes glowing, Crystal told little Hope, "I love you," and then she looked at the Holets and said, "Take care of her for me."

After Hope was born and this story made national news,

the Mending Fences drug treatment program in Florida reached out to Crystal in New Mexico. The facility sent Kat McLaughlin, a recovering heroin addict, to convince Crystal to overcome her drug addiction and start a new life. McLaughlin described Crystal's situation as one of the worst she had ever seen. "She was completely hopeless," McLaughlin said, "using the hardest drugs in the most extreme ways."

Crystal went to Florida with McLaughlin, entered the treatment program, got clean and sober, and started living on her own off the streets. Officer Holets continued to speak regularly with Crystal on the phone to tell her of her daughter's progress and to give Crystal ongoing encouragement and support.

Regarding her daughter, Crystal said, "Hope is in a great place, and I trust and have faith that she's going to have a beautiful life."

Strive to Make a Difference

Several aspects of a professional life of public service are spiritual — meaning they are an expression and affirmation of goodness, selflessness, integrity, compassion, helpfulness, and loving service. Spirituality refers to that which positively affects one's inner spirit in ways that are enriching, inspiring, and life-enabling. In order to maintain essential spiritual wellness and resilience, peace officers need to be driven by their heart to make a meaningful difference in their agency, with their colleagues, in the community, and for those they serve. This spiritual component of selfless service is essential for work to be meaningful, productive of wellness, and life-affirming. This inherent spiritual aspect of service is what enhances resilience, keeps us motivated, makes work more meaningful and purposeful, and helps keep us well and at peace.

The conscious choices we make and the ways we choose to handle every call for service affect the shape and form that life (and work) will take, both for ourselves and for everyone affected by our thoughts, words, and actions.

Consciousness and spirituality are two sides of the same coin. The spiritual elements of consciousness that consistently produce the most positive effects in our wellness and resilience are selflessness, generosity, compassion, kindness, understanding, humility, service to others, and gratitude. When these aspects of spiritual consciousness are cultivated and become consistently part of our service, we stand the greatest chance of not only maintaining but improving our health, wellness, and peace, as well as our influence with others.

The critical problem for peace officers is that the everyday traumas of the job erode their ability to be consciously aware and spiritual in their service. The trauma they experience can gradually, over time, suffocate their hearts. When the heart is suffocating, we can become calloused and uncaring, disengaged with life, inactive, self-centered, less resilient, disinterested in trying to make a difference, and unhealthy. This is what makes so many peace officers cynical, angry, frustrated, intensely negative, and unable to maintain close and meaningful relationships.

The good news is that we can reverse the negative influences of trauma by proactively, consciously activating the tremendous healing capacity of our heart — purposefully putting our heart into our work, regardless of the outcome. The essential principle to remember is to *consistently make the intentional, conscious effort to make a positive difference in all aspects of your service.* If you do this, your heart will respond and resist shutting down.

During a recent presentation of my emotional survival and wellness training class, a probation officer from Northern California told me how she had become very disillusioned and indifferent after her failed efforts to help a juvenile offender. The seventeen-year-old male had been sent to juvenile hall for a series of robberies. This officer interacted with him numerous times every day over the nine months he was incarcerated.

The probation officer felt a connection to this young man and went out of her way every chance she had to speak with him, to offer advice and help, and to try to change his life. They had several very positive interactions. Because of these, she looked forward every morning to going back to work, something she hadn't felt in years.

Tragically, less than a month after his release from custody, the juvenile was killed in a gang fight. Tears filled her eyes as she told me and the class this story and how it made her feel like nothing extra she did would ever make a difference — so why try anymore?

This is a critical concept to understand: The potential outcomes of our efforts to serve with a purposeful heart are extremely varied, and ultimately *they do not matter*. We have absolutely no control over outcomes. We have influence during the moment at hand, and hopefully a lasting influence, but we have absolutely no control over the choices others make or the outcome of circumstances.

What's vital to understand is that what matters is our conscious intention and effort *in the moment* to serve with purposeful compassion. When we do that, we can erase some of our past traumas, embody our purpose, feel better, and enrich our spirit. During those nine months while she was giving herself in her service, that probation officer did make a difference both within herself and in unknown ways with the offender. In itself, that was healing, positive, and helpful. The fact that the juvenile decided to later make further bad choices and waste his life does not negate the officer's efforts to make a difference.

It is *the conscious effort to do good and to make a difference in the present moment* that is essential. If we never make that effort, then absolutely no added good will ever come to us or to anyone else from our service.

Evaluating the Best Choice in the Moment

We are all capable of transcending the self-centered, negative aspects of human nature and acting in ways that embody the universal spiritual qualities of selfless service, compassion, and helpfulness. Purposed, spiritually conscious service involves idealism and the great nobility of what it means to protect and serve.

Peace officers protect and enable life, keep the peace, and prevent others from becoming victims of crime, natural disasters, and evil. Every day, in everything we think, say, and do, we have countless opportunities to positively influence others. The more spiritually conscious and aware we are, the more our influence will be positive, constructive, and helpful, both to others as well as to our own health and wellness.

Nearly every waking moment, we are constantly making choices, many without even thinking about them. The more consciously aware we become of the choices we are making in even the small details of our life, the better our choices will be and the more influential we can be in creating positive change.

No matter what the situation, there are always several options of how to respond; that's what makes it a choice. So among all the potential options, look for the choice that is the most compassionate, life-affirming, and productive of wellness. By consistently and consciously striving to choose the most compassionate and life-affirming options available, we will always help promote wellness, increase our resilience, and improve our sense of peace, fulfillment, satisfaction, and motivation. Here is a closer look at each of these aspects.

Compassionate

The one lesson I learned more than any other in nearly thirty years of police service is that police work is truly a vocation of the heart. If someone is not driven by their heart to make that positive difference, then the job is likely going to eat them alive.

Being a peace officer boils down to the desire to serve, to help, to protect, to give of ourselves through compassionate actions because people, and our community, matter to us — *and they need to always matter.* Whether it's making an arrest or working to solve someone's problem, wanting people to be protected and to experience improvements in their lives should always be our concern. It is a way of serving not only our country, but our community and our greater human family. Our service is an expression of love: love of country; love of peace, freedom, and security; love of family and neighbors; love of our brother and sister human beings; and love of community.

Serving with compassion through acts of kindness, caring, and support means we are consciously trying to make a difference in every call, whether it is taking a petty theft report or investigating a violent rape or robbery; whether it is speaking with a colleague or interacting with a member of the community; or whether it's making countless arrests. Compassionate and helpful actions are essential because that is what heals and feeds our heart, that nourishes, inspires, and sustains it. That is what will keep you interested, engaged with life, able to relate to others in more meaningful ways, and increasingly able to not only survive but thrive in your career.

Compassion is the DNA of service. The peace officer profession is dedicated to relieving suffering, to serving the needs of others no matter who they may be, to standing up to evil, to solving problems, and to creating positive change in people's lives. We don't always get the chance to save a life, but every day we get numerous opportunities to affect a life. The more that we act in purposeful and positive ways reflective of spiritual values, the more we create wellness.

By serving with compassion and a purposeful heart, I in no way am implying that we should not arrest people nor use reasonable force when needed. Those are of course essential elements of the job, but so is doing whatever we can to help solve a problem and to do whatever good we can. We also should be tolerant and understanding and treat people with dignity and respect.

Serving with compassion means we are purposefully promoting the greatest good. It means trying to be helpful beyond what is needed just to handle the call. It means intentionally helping in any ways that are needed.

Compassionate service means trying to make a difference because you care about people and about the good you can potentially do; you care about the image of your agency, the professionalism of your service, your integrity and honor, and your influence to create positive change.

Serving with your heart and acting with compassion have many scientifically proven benefits, which include the following:

- reduced stress levels
- activation of the pleasure centers in the brain

- increased resilience and the ability to cope
- positive mood
- increased motivation and job satisfaction
- enhanced overall mental and physical health
- lessened depression and anxiety
- increased ability to connect with and relate to others
- enhanced longevity and survivability

Being purposeful through heart-centered service erases a lot of the negative influences of trauma and acute stress, which enhances overall wellness and resilience. Because all life is connected, what benefits others benefits us. When you are doing something good for another, you are in fact doing something good for yourself.

★ "A Cop's Most Disarming Weapon: ★
Compassion"

On June 6, 2021, correspondent Steve Hartman from CBS *Sunday Morning* produced this three-minute video, which highlights several peace officers who made a significant difference in people's lives while serving from a heart of compassion.

https://www.youtube.com/watch?v=_hncPj1lQ44&t=1s
Courtesy of CBS *Sunday Morning* — Steve Hartman

★

Life-Affirming

In order to take the more life-affirming course of action, we have to consciously want to be life-affirming. By *life-affirming*, I mean choices that do the following:

- add to your peace rather than take away from it
- enhance your health and wellness rather than deplete them
- increase your joy and sense of fulfillment
- provide meaning and a sense of positive, constructive service

Compassionate choices are also usually the most life-affirming — in part by affirming the good in ourselves. If our choices are not compassionate and life-affirming, then they can erode our resilience, motivation, energies, enjoyment, peace, and wellness. Significantly, they can also erode our ability to care and be useful. This of course leads to the potential cancers of the peace officer profession: indifference, disengagement, callousness, and disconnection from others.

Productive of Wellness

If everything we do is both compassionate and life-affirming, then our actions will be productive of wellness. We cannot be well and resilient when we are not practicing the vital components that are essential for enhancing our health and well-being.

The habits, thought patterns, and negative beliefs that are so natural to many peace officers can slowly destroy their ability to create a foundation of inner wellness and peace. This includes dismissive responses to certain persons; the negative emotions of anger, fear, resentment, and judgment; being un-forgiving; thinking negatively; and not being proactive about increasing our physical, mental, emotional, and spiritual well-ness. All of these greatly diminish our capacity to thrive and survive in our profession.

The remedy to all of this is to *become more consciously aware and purposeful in our choices to be more compassionate and life-affirming.* I know this is real and is tremendously effec-tive, not only because I have lived it and seen how it has saved my career and life, but because I've seen it work for countless others.

The undeniable secret to not only surviving a peace officer career but loving it and remaining healthy and well through-out one's career is to be driven by a spiritual heart to make a difference, to create positive change, to alleviate suffering, and to be useful to others. The surest way to increase survivability, work through trauma, and enjoy a greater quality of life in a service career is to make compassion and life-affirming actions as natural as breathing.

This is what is described so vividly and movingly in the in-spiring book *Man's Search for Meaning by Viktor Frankl* (which I discuss in "Seek Meaning and Purpose," pages 51–52). The prisoners in the Nazi concentration camps who managed to overcome their own despair and hopelessness tended to be those who focused on others. The sense of purpose they found by helping others, by acting on their love for others through selfless giving, sustained them even in the midst of their own terrible suffering.

According to Frankl, our emotional well-being and sur-vival depend on our ability to find meaning in our lives greater than satisfying our own self-interest. We do this by practicing life-affirming compassion daily, which is also the key to surviving and thriving throughout your own career of service as a peace officer.

The Spiritual Nature of Service

Thomas Jefferson beautifully expressed in our Declaration of Independence that all persons are created equal and are endowed by their creator with certain inalienable rights — life, liberty, and the pursuit of happiness. The United States is unique in the world in declaring that such rights are sacred and are given to all equally from God, which is why the Constitution enshrines the fundamental precept that no government can ever take them away without due process. The police have been entrusted by the people to secure these God-given rights.

There is an inherent spirituality in service and in being responsible for the protection of life and our sacred rights. Such spirituality is expressed through our highest motives and selfless desire to go beyond our self-interest to give ourselves in the service of others — and many would add, in the service of God.

As a peace officer, I find that having faith in the concept of a universal presence of goodness, or of the guiding hand of God, is extremely helpful and even inescapable. Though peace officers deal with danger, violence, depravity, and suffering on a daily basis, the pledge of our profession is to do good by protecting others and society. This embodies the main purpose of any spiritual practice or religious faith, which is to bring people to a more perfect union with each other and with the divine source of life. Thus, any spiritual or religious practice can be comforting and inspiring to a first responder, offering support, guidance, understanding, purpose, healing, and peace. It can help us maintain a positive perspective in our work life and provide coping mechanisms to positively process emotional and psychological trauma. It offers a shield for our spirit.

If a particular faith or spiritual practice is or was once a part of your life, nurture it and use it for your well-being. The spiritual values of service are inspired by a source beyond human intellect. They run contrary to the selfish interests of mere survival. They are the very values that make life, and a life of service, meaningful. For many who serve, the wellspring of these spiritual values is a source that creates and gives life. I believe that if we ignore that which gives life, our lives and service will be adversely affected in many ways.

Our inner spirit is the foundation of life, for it comprises our capacity to love, to be resilient, to cope, to do good, to live with integrity and character, to keep a clean conscience, and to remain motivated. It is the foundation of our overall health and wellness.

Our inner spirit is assaulted constantly by the daily traumas we experience at work, and it is those spiritual values that restore, renew, inspire, and heal our inner spirit. The spiritual aspect of ourselves provides the foundation for a life of service. As Helen Keller once said, "The best and most beautiful things in the world cannot be seen or even touched, but just felt in the heart."

The negative elements of human nature — which include envy, jealousy, unbridled ambition, pride, revenge, selfishness, unforgiveness, anger, and so on — are all poisonous to our inner spirit and our ability to be well and resilient. The more we make the conscious effort to express the spiritual nature of service, the healthier we will be and the more good we will be able to do. Remaining connected to the spiritual nature of service has been the single greatest influence that enabled me to work in law enforcement for thirty years while remaining healthy, positive, motivated, and at peace.

Coping with Suffering

All peace officers can find it very difficult to deal with the suffering of others. First responders are always in the middle of heartache. These senseless tragedies, however, provide countless opportunities to try to make a difference by listening, offering hope, or filling a need. Sometimes all a peace officer can do is listen, be understanding and compassionate, and find a few kind words that might offer hope.

It's always difficult seeing people suffer. At times, officers can find it hard not to suffer with them. To avoid this pain, some of us fall into the trap of shutting down emotionally. In the process we lose some of ourselves and become emotionally calloused — not feeling things anymore and being indifferent, disengaged, and emotionally dead inside. Emotional apathy is very difficult to recover from, and it can affect every aspect of someone's personal life. Being so affected, we don't feel joy with our kids or close with our spouse. That's always a potential hazard of the job, given what we experience every day.

By focusing on the spiritual aspect of service, by trying to help and do good in whatever ways you can, you can hopefully avoid becoming overwhelmed by the suffering of others. The more you look for opportunities to be helpful and useful, the more resilience you are likely to have.

As Marianne Williamson writes, "Spirituality reflects the most sophisticated mindset, and the most powerful force available for the transformation of human suffering."

Remember Positive Outcomes

Over the years I've had people come into the police department and thank me for arresting them. Because of their arrest, they were finally able to get off drugs, or the shock of being arrested gave them the impetus to turn their life around. Those instances remind me of why we are so needed and all the potential good we can do with each encounter.

There is a fundamental principle regarding all the good we do and its long-lasting effects on our health and well-being: *Focusing on the positive makes the negative lose its power.* Imagine a ledger that is divided in half. On the right side is a list of every bad, negative, stressful, and traumatic experience you've had at work. On the left side, envision a list of all the good you have been able to do through compassionate service. Every good, positive item on the left side of the ledger automatically erases some of the bad experiences on the right — *as far as their potential negative effects upon you.*

That's just how the mind works. Good, selfless service to others erases a lot of past trauma. I know it to be an absolute fact; I have lived it and seen it, and it is backed up by science. Make a pledge to yourself to reach retirement without needing to spend your time trying to forget all the bad because it is outweighed by all the good you were able to accomplish.

In the early 2000s, four men were going around suburban San Diego getting homeless men drunk and then having them fight each other for more beer. The result was a notorious and wildly popular set of videos entitled *Bumfights.* The four men made hundreds of thousands of dollars selling these videos. The homeless men were often badly injured in the fights, including broken bones and concussions.

Everyone in the police department knew what was going

on, but no one thought it was a crime. I looked into the matter and searched for something we could arrest the "filmmakers" for, since the homeless men were being cruelly victimized and seriously hurt — even hospitalized.

After researching the penal code, I found an obscure crime no one had ever heard of before — *instigating two people to fight other than an authorized state prize fight*. This law, enacted in 1872, was intended primarily to prevent underground boxing matches. In this case, since more than one filmmaker was involved and working together, it made the alleged crime a felony — conspiracy to conduct an unauthorized prize fight. After a four-month investigation, the filmmakers were arrested, charged, and subsequently convicted.

Then a miracle occurred. One of the homeless men, Rufus Hannah, had been a chronic drunk since the age of twelve. Hannah was in his late forties when *Bumfights* started. When the organizers were arrested and prosecuted, a citizen came forward and took Hannah under his care. He'd seen the homeless man in his neighborhood and was so moved by his plight that he took it upon himself to help out. As a result, Hannah got clean and sober, he cowrote a 2011 book about his life (entitled *A Bum Deal*), and he started lecturing on college campuses about homelessness and alcoholism. He even visited the state capitol to speak with legislators about these problems. His turnaround was the most dramatic I had seen in thirty years of law enforcement. Because we tried to make a difference, this man was given a new life and then himself helped many people. Tragically, Hannah died in a car crash in 2017.

The potential effects of being driven by your heart to make a difference through the inherent spirituality of service can be tremendous and far-reaching — and it can produce a ripple effect with positive results well beyond your initial actions. Strive to be purposeful in your service, consciously committed to always choosing to be both compassionate and life-affirming, and your actions will be productive of wellness and resilience.

Self-Awareness Questions

- How compassionate and life-affirming are your choices and your service right now?
- How much do you care about the suffering of those who are mentally ill, drug addicted, or homeless or who have had intensely traumatic childhoods?
- In what ways can you be more purposeful in serving with your heart and trying to make a difference?
- What positive changes can you make in your agency, with your colleagues, and in the community you serve?
- What specific things can you do to practice the spiritual elements of service to be more useful and helpful, loving, selfless, and understanding?

Case Study: Trying to Be Helpful

Officers Janet Lee and Tom Gray are at a domestic violence call. They and other officers have responded to this address numerous times, and the couple is always fighting, yelling, and screaming at each other. The officers quickly ascertain that there was no assault and no crime has been committed, and in their frustration, they try to leave as soon as they can. Neither officer has any interest in trying to help the couple; they just want them to shut up and not bother the neighbors. So they tell the couple to quiet down, and then they leave.

Case Study Reflection

In order to make a difference, you first have to *want to*. Over the years, many officers shut down emotionally and don't really care anymore. They forget why they became peace officers in the first place. That's the issue with the two officers in this scenario.

Rather than leave as soon as possible, the officers should ask themselves: *What good can we do here? How can we be help-ful? How can we make a positive difference?* Simply by asking these questions with a genuine desire to do good, your intu-ition will go to work and constructive ideas will come.

For instance, the officers might take the time to speak to each person separately and find out why they keep fighting. More might be going on than is obvious, and the officers could explore potential options to address each person's specific prob-lems. That might involve providing information on battered women's shelters, substance abuse treatment, couples counseling or conflict resolution, individual therapy, or anger management. If the officers were proactive, they might have already created a list of local nonprofits and community programs that provide low-cost help. Of course, the couple has to solve their own prob-lems, but by trying to help, the officers will know for themselves that they've done what they could, which preserves their own well-being. And if their intervention works, it means one less domestic violence call to have to worry about.

Caring for Those Who Don't Care for Themselves

When people are too self-destructive, drug addicted, crazed, ignorant, or hateful to care for themselves, why should we care? When people are the cause of their own problems and don't make any effort to help themselves, why should we help them?

This is a question anyone might ask, but peace officers have a unique obligation. Peace officers are empowered by the people of their community and state to keep the peace, to treat *everyone* with equal justice and concern, to protect all life (not just the lives of those we like), to solve problems within the community, and to be responsive to quality-of-life issues. An integral aspect of a peace officer's job is to protect, serve, and help where possible (which may include arresting) those who are either too drunk, too crazed, too addicted, too hopeless, too helpless, or too ignorant to help themselves.

As the stories in this chapter show, you never know what good can result when you are actively trying to make a difference. Sometimes no outward good will come about, but at other times, it does. We have people's lives in our hands; people depend upon us to be concerned and to do the right thing. We are expected to be fair and helpful and to try our best no matter what the outcome.

For a moment, imagine the suffering and despair of those who can no longer help themselves: those who are addicted to drugs and alcohol; who have had their children taken away; who have experienced nothing since birth except neglect, violence, molestation, and fear. Imagine what it would be like to have been raised in a gang culture or to live in a home where violence and depravity are normal. None of that excuses someone's own hurtful behavior. Everyone needs to be held accountable for the harm they have caused. But no matter how far people fall, they are still human beings. We should try to alleviate suffering whenever and wherever we can. The influence you wield always has the potential to significantly affect someone's life in a positive way for both them and the community.

Chapter Six

---★---

Posttraumatic Stress and Ways to Heal

Everybody can be great... because anybody can serve.
You don't have to have a college degree to serve. You only need
a heart full of grace. A soul generated by love.
— MARTIN LUTHER KING JR.

Being a peace officer inherently exposes you to repeated and significant traumatic incidents and acute stress. It is impossible to avoid events that can potentially injure the brain and cause posttraumatic stress. Every day you experience varied traumas that have the potential to negatively affect you in significant ways over a long period of time. The highly toxic and cumulative nature of trauma eats away at resilience, peace, health, and well-being. For this reason, it's essential to learn how to prepare yourself to constructively process the repeated trauma of your profession and how to heal.

Posttraumatic stress brain injuries are brought about by continued exposure to tragedies, extremely disturbing experiences, or psychological trauma causing intense fear, horror, or helplessness. Death, the suffering of others, violence, injuries, suicides, child molestation and abuse, dangers, and threats are all forms of trauma that can shock and alter how the brain functions. Every peace officer is susceptible to these potentially debilitating injuries, but there are ways to prepare for and process trauma that can significantly reduce the intensity and duration of symptoms, if not heal them altogether.

Posttraumatic Stress Symptoms and How They Develop

During or after a traumatic incident (or after experiencing several traumas), someone may experience emotional numbing, the inability to recall information or details related to the incident, the feeling of being in a fog, depression, and a repeated sense of watching themselves from a distance. They may also feel intense anxieties, fears, and uncontrollable emotions with intrusive thoughts.

Well after the incident(s), sufferers may reexperience trauma through flashbacks, night terrors, or illusions — seeing things that are not real or are not happening, yet are experienced as real. Physical symptoms of posttraumatic stress injuries may include an extremely heightened sense of hypervigilance along with an inability to relax, extreme anxiety, serious difficulty sleeping, and intense agitation. Officers may also try to avoid any reminder of the critical incident by staying clear of certain people or locations, switching shifts, or not coming to work. They may even experience inadvertent incidents of dereliction of duty.

Other potential symptoms include significant mood disturbances. Someone may feel disconnected from others and unable to express feelings in the way they did previously. They may have wide-ranging emotions they have never experienced before and that seemingly come from nowhere. They could experience angry rages, the inability to concentrate or focus, an exaggerated startle response, issues with intimacy, continued depression, and the inability to stop mentally replaying the traumatic event over and over. Past traumas might also flood the mind.

These symptoms tend to have a profound negative effect on work performance and overall quality of life. They often lead to poor coping skills or to risk-taking behaviors, such as excessive drinking, drug use (legal and illegal), promiscuity and affairs, and various addictions, such as gambling, pornography, pills, and others. Other signs of maladaptive coping include difficulties in family relationships and an excessive desire to isolate oneself.

If you ever experience any of these symptoms, the key is to realize that *all of them are natural, normal physiological reactions as the mind attempts to process trauma*, since the brain's normal processing ability has been injured. People experience these symptoms in different combinations and to greater or lesser degrees, but every peace officer is susceptible to sustaining a posttraumatic stress injury and its symptoms. The most important thing to remember is that it is critical to recognize these symptoms, tell someone, and seek help if needed. Most symptoms do not just go away on their own, and severe symptoms usually require the intervention of professional trauma therapy, such as EMDR (see "EMDR Therapy," pages 119–122).

The first step is the simplest but can feel like the most difficult: telling someone you trust, "Something's going on inside I don't like. I might need some help." Not asking for help kills more officers than anything else.

Resisting or hiding the symptoms can inadvertently cause symptoms to worsen and become seriously life altering. Ignoring symptoms will not make them suddenly go away. We need to be trained in advance to deal with them or helped through the experience. That way, our minds can positively and effectively place the trauma in the proper perspective and, by doing so, alleviate the symptoms and release the trauma.

There is never any shame in needing or seeking help; it is normal and should become expected for every peace officer. In fact, as a matter of emotional survival and wellness maintenance, I believe peace officers should see a certified trauma professional (preferably one certified in EMDR) annually who is experienced in peace officer trauma — even if officers are not experiencing any symptoms. This would be like going to a medical doctor for an annual physical checkup.

The only shame is not doing everything we can to be well; to enjoy life, family, and work; and to move forward. It would be a tragedy to choose to suffer through something that reduces the quality of life when there is assistance available that has been proven effective. Posttraumatic stress is not about what's wrong with you — it is about what has *happened* to you, and those injuries and symptoms can be healed or at least mitigated.

Preparation: Mitigating the Effects of Trauma

To increase resilience, limit the intensity of posttraumatic stress symptoms, and constructively process trauma, preparation is key. This means practicing wellness strategies daily to strengthen mental, physical, emotional, and spiritual resilience. This will provide you with the best chance of avoiding such injuries or being able to move through them. In addition to the wellness strategies detailed in chapter 3, the following will help you prepare for and mitigate the effects of trauma.

Set Up a Support System

Develop and maintain a trusted support system of family and friends. Discuss with loved ones what to expect, how you are likely to behave after a critical incident — either after a traumatic event or after consistent exposures to significant stress — and how they can best support and most effectively help you. Remember, your health and quality of life depend on your level of preparedness, the development of an effective support system, and your willingness to talk with people. Tell the people closest to you what you need from them.

★ "1997 N. Hollywood Shootout" ★

This video contains about 2.5 minutes of a 45-minute active shootout that occurred in North Hollywood, California, in 1997. Two bank robbers held up a Bank of America wearing body armor from head to toe and carrying AK-47s. They got into a running gun battle with the police, firing over a thousand rounds at them. They shot and critically wounded eleven officers, but ultimately, the only two people who died were the bank robbers.

As you watch and listen to the radio traffic, imagine yourself in the middle of this horrendous traumatic experience. Think about how it might affect you, possibly for the rest of your life. Think about how you would respond to such trauma. Think about what support systems you already have in place and the various ways

---

you can cultivate resilience and support *before* something like this happens to you.

I want to stress that most peace officers will never experience any single incident this extremely violent and traumatic in their career. Any officer might — every day at work holds that possibility — but chances are they won't. *However, every officer will absolutely experience an equivalent amount of accumulated trauma over the course of their careers.* Those traumatic experiences will be spread out in smaller doses over a twenty- or thirty-year career — another dead kid, another suicide, another fight for your life, another dangerous situation, another senseless act of violence, another child molestation, another violent sexual assault, another crazed deranged person, and so on. These traumas add up to potentially affect someone the same as if they were involved in a forty-five-minute shootout. That's why it's so imperative to practice wellness and resilience strategies every day, with every call for service, to prevent an accumulation of trauma.

https://www.youtube.com/watch?v=ZttwYwIIelI
Courtesy of LiveLeak

★

Get an Annual Emotional Survival and Wellness Checkup

As a form of prevention and wellness maintenance, consult with a trauma professional specializing in treating first responders and trauma (using EMDR) to determine if you are being adversely affected by past trauma and to gain insight into how to deal with trauma and stress more effectively.

The idea behind an annual checkup like this is *not* that "something is wrong." Something may or may not be affecting you, but the emphasis is on getting a wellness check and discussing the previous year — both professionally and personally — as a preventative and wellness-maintenance measure.

Mentally Rehearse Your Trauma Response

Recognize that you may very well one day experience a significant traumatic incident like the Bank of America shootout, and develop the mindset that you will survive. Envision how you will handle such an experience both during and after the fact. What might help you process the trauma and place it in its proper perspective? Mental rehearsal and visualization — seeing yourself experiencing a traumatic incident and coming through it all right — is important. This visualization is important even if you are never involved in a major critical incident, since the same wellness preparation will help you cope with all of the smaller daily traumas that every officer is constantly exposed to.

Practice Tactical Breathing

According to Lieutenant Colonel David Grossman (coauthor of *Warrior Mindset* and *On Combat*), tactical breathing can dramatically help people not only function at the highest levels during a traumatic event but also cope with the aftermath. Essentially, tactical breathing consists of the following: Just before or after a traumatic incident, or whenever your mind is reliving the event, take a deep, slow breath in through your nose, hold it as long as you can, then even more slowly breathe out of your mouth. Repeat this several times. This will calm and center the automatic stress responses of your mind and body and help you recover faster. As your body and mind calm down, your brain becomes more capable of processing trauma so that hopefully there won't be any long-lasting effects.

Don't Postpone Professional Assistance

Shortly after a serious critical incident, seek assistance from a trauma professional who has experience in traumatic events, whether you think you need it or not. Most agencies have a contract with such psychologists (through the employee assistance program) and offer a certain number of confidential visits for free or at a significantly reduced cost. Treatments for trauma and posttraumatic stress injuries can be relatively short-term and extremely effective (such as EMDR), especially if sought soon after an incident. However, it is never too late to seek help and to heal from trauma. With professional help, you will hopefully be able to regain control and work through your symptoms without them upsetting your life.

Two extremely useful, twenty-four-hour call centers are CopLine (800-267-5463) and Safe Call Now (206-459-3020); websites for both are listed in the Resources. These confidential hotlines are staffed by highly trained and vetted retired peace officers who have been through it all and want to give back to their peers who are still serving. These competent, confident, committed, and compassionate retired officers have experienced the stress and traumas of police work, know how these can impact individuals and families, and understand what it takes to make it to the other side. Further, these hotlines maintain complete confidentiality and anonymity (if desired) and have earned the trust of the law enforcement community. The call centers have no connection to any police agency, will not report anything said to anyone, and will not even ask for your name or anything about you unless you want to offer it. They also provide referrals for other support services.

Keep Yourself Well Hydrated

Develop the habit of consistently being well hydrated — with water, not energy drinks, coffee, or sports drinks. Maintaining good hydration helps the brain remain alert and able to process trauma more effectively. Good hydration coupled with good sleep management, consistent exercise, and a well-balanced diet will significantly help you be prepared for trauma and will lessen its effects.

Discuss the Incident

After a traumatic incident, find understanding people to talk with who will listen without judgment. Peer-support colleagues who have experienced traumatic events offer an invaluable, confidential, and trusted resource. They are individuals you can talk with to begin the healing process.

After the Injury: Symptoms and Treatments

Posttraumatic stress is a complex injury to the brain's coping ability in which the affected person's memory, emotional responses, intellectual processes, and nervous system are all disrupted. Such injuries and symptoms can occur immediately or weeks or years after a critical traumatic incident or an accumulation of incidents. Approximately 25 percent of those experiencing posttraumatic stress have a delayed onset of symptoms. Up to 80 percent of people with posttraumatic stress also develop other serious health issues, including depression, anxieties, alcohol and substance abuse, heart disease, and diabetes. You and your family should be vigilant to watch for all the symptoms described in this chapter.

Many times a person suffering from posttraumatic stress injuries does not realize what has happened or how they have changed. If family members or coworkers see some of these signs, it is critical for them to ask questions and offer help. Coworkers and family can assist the person in seeking help in a positive way, by supporting and showing genuine concern for the affected person's well-being without judging, criticizing, or pressuring the person to just "get over it."

The following nonintrusive, nonjudgmental questions can be used to begin a conversation:

- "The other day I noticed that you weren't really yourself. Has anything been bothering you?"
- "Do you want to get some coffee to catch up? I've noticed over the past few weeks that you haven't been yourself."
- "I'm concerned about you — how are you doing? If you ever need to talk or need anything at all, I'm here for you."

There are several effective treatments for posttraumatic stress, but in my opinion and that of many other trauma professionals, EMDR is the most powerful and best suited for peace officers.

EMDR Therapy

EMDR — which stands for eye movement desensitization and reprocessing — has been practiced for over thirty years and been endorsed by the World Health Organization and the International Association of Chiefs of Police. The military has been using EMDR for years to help heal soldiers returning home from war zones, and there are currently over twenty thousand EMDR-certified trauma professionals in the United States.

EMDR is a way to reboot the brain and restore its normal functioning — and this can be done within a relatively short period of time, only a few sessions, despite the severity of the trauma or the symptoms. The theory behind it is that traumatic experiences upset the biochemical balance of the brain. EMDR is a form of accelerated information processing that tends to unblock the brain's information-processing system. EMDR allows for the brain to complete the processing that was left unfinished after the shock of a traumatic event, which can injure or alter the brain's normal processing. EMDR desensitizes the event and allows the brain to file the experience in memory without the distressing thoughts and emotions that were intertwined with that fractured memory. Once the brain has been rebooted, it can function more normally to process the trauma.

As I've mentioned, I had EMDR therapy, and something that had bothered me for twenty-five years went away after only two sessions. I could not recommend it strongly enough. It is extremely effective. It is *not* talk therapy, but a very specific method for rebooting the brain to regain normal functioning. More likely than not, you will experience some or complete relief of your symptoms; many people report improvement after only a dozen sessions or less. In my travels around the country teaching, I have never heard one negative thing about EMDR. Typically, people say, "It's the best thing that ever happened to me. I should have done it years ago. It saved my life. I never thought I could feel this good again."

That said, this extremely effective therapy can be exhausting and emotionally draining in the short term, but overall it's a relatively easy process by which many or all of the negative, dark emotions and thoughts associated with traumatic memories become disassociated and released. You still remember the incidents, but they no longer adversely affect you. The healing effects tend to be permanent. EMDR is just as effective even if you can't pinpoint a particular traumatic incident as the source of your symptoms, as is often the case.

The purpose of EMDR is to enable a mental restructuring of information about the traumatic event that has not been resolved and normally processed. It helps eliminate the surge of emotion that an individual experiences when thinking about or talking about the event.

The following true story, told to me by a San Diego police officer, is a great example of how effective EMDR can be.

I was involved in a fatal shooting on duty and killed the suspect. I was fine for about six months afterward. Then, one day I came home from work and my five-year-old son came running up to greet me as he always does. For just a split moment, I suddenly saw a flash of my son's face covered in blood as if he were bleeding to death. The vision disappeared as fast as it had come. It was very startling to me, but I just shrugged it off.

A few more days went by and I was fine. Then, I came home, and I had the same horrible vision of "seeing" blood all over my son's face. It looked absolutely real and I couldn't get the image out of my mind. I panicked, my heart was racing and pounding out of my chest, and I was terror-stricken. I still can't believe how real it looked. I even reached toward his face to try to wipe all the blood away.

For several months from then on, every time I looked at my son I saw a severe head wound and his entire head drenched in blood. Every time I looked at him my brain and my eyes were telling me, "He's dying. Do something. He's bleeding to death."

I then started seeing blood all over the place — a pool of blood in the shower, blood on the dinner table and in my food, blood on the bedsheets underneath my wife's head as if she were bleeding out while she slept, and all over my hands. Often when I looked at my hands, I saw them covered in blood. I could even feel the stickiness of it. I would wash my hands multiple times, but I saw that they were still covered in blood, and I could still feel it.

It became impossible for me to sleep. I was always in a panic. I thought I was losing my mind. I didn't want to tell my wife because I didn't want her to think I was going crazy. I just thought it would eventually go away, but it didn't. I would even close my eyes and tell myself, "My son is not injured. He's fine. I'm just seeing phantom blood. *Everything is okay." I would then open my eyes, see all the blood, and be terrified as if he were dying. I learned that you can't talk your way out of what your brain is telling you is real.*

Over the months I became more desperate and was hopelessly depressed. I began to contemplate suicide because I felt so hopeless and helpless. I realized that if I did take my own life, I wouldn't really be ending any suffering. I'd just be spreading it around to the people I love the most.

In desperation I confided in a peer-support officer at my agency, one who had been in a shooting himself. This officer told me about EMDR, which I had never heard of before. He told me it was a way to heal and to get my life back. Then he said, "Just commit to three sessions and evaluate it after that if you want to have more. It won't make your symptoms any worse." That convinced me to try it.

Well, I stopped going after two sessions because I have never seen phantom blood again. It saved my life. It's been a few years since that experience, and I still have never seen phantom blood, not even once. EMDR is an incredible treatment that can heal your traumas and restore your life. Remember it throughout your career. Do it regularly whenever something is going on inside that you don't like.

To learn more, visit the EMDR International Association (www.emdria.org), and use Google to find a certified EMDR trauma therapist in your area.

★ "EMDR: Eye Movement Desensitization ★
and Reprocessing"

In this excellent three-minute video, a trauma professional who has practiced EMDR for over twenty-five years explains the technique. The video includes officer testimonials.

https://www.youtube.com/watch?v=xhnKBmOZi3Q
Courtesy of LegacyProductions.org

★

Self-Awareness Questions

List the reasons why you would not seek help to heal if you were suffering from posttraumatic stress symptoms. Then list all the reasons why you should seek help to heal. Which are more important to you?

Case Study: Recognizing the Signs

For several months, Officer Cameron notices that a fellow officer doesn't seem himself. The officer has become withdrawn, much quieter, and distant. Officer Cameron asks him if everything is all right, and the officer says he's fine.

Over the next few weeks, Officer Cameron sees no change and is becoming more concerned. He asks for a meeting with the officer out in the field, alone. While they're talking, the troubled officer makes a joke about hurting himself and immediately laughs it off, saying he'd never do something like that. Officer Cameron decides that, if the officer can joke about suicide, he must not be serious, so he drops it. Officer Cameron doesn't want to make the officer mad or embarrass him by assuming he needs help.

Case Study Reflection

I know of an officer whose best friend, another officer, killed himself. My friend strongly advises, and this is corroborated by mental health professionals, that the very first moment you get the idea that someone may be thinking of killing themselves, take it seriously, be genuinely concerned, and be direct with them. Ask them right away, "I'm concerned about you. Are you thinking of hurting yourself?" Be direct and honest with people; don't hesitate.

Even if the officer denies it or gets upset and angry that you bring it up, ask anyway. It's impossible to put the idea of suicide into someone's head. If someone is considering it, they have most likely been thinking about it for months before anyone ever notices.

Further, even if the person does shrug you off, they know that you care enough to notice and reach out. That might be all they need to keep themselves from going through with a suicide attempt. They know at least one person cares and has offered to help, and so you might be the person they call in the middle of the night.

Of course, if an officer does admit to having suicidal thoughts, offer any support and help that you can. Ask if it's all right for you to tell a peer-support colleague, who can provide resources and keep in touch with the officer as well.

Tragic things happen sometimes when good people notice or sense something is wrong but do nothing. In this profession we're all united by trauma. Therefore, we're uniquely situated to support and help our brothers and sisters that serve by our side.

Fears about Confidentiality

Many peace officers have natural concerns about confidentiality. If they go to a trauma professional, how can they be certain that the visit and what they discuss will remain confidential and not be told to the police department?

In my experience, these worries are entirely unfounded. It is unlawful for any health practitioner, psychologist, psychiatrist, agency chaplain, or trauma professional to divulge any information whatsoever about clients. The only exceptions to this are when someone discloses that they are about to kill others or commit some other crime; in these extremely rare cases, professionals are mandated to report these statements. However, if you still worry that visits with professionals connected to your agency's employee assistance program (EAP) will not be kept confidential, then go to a trauma professional who is not associated with your agency and use your own personal insurance to cover it.

As a captain, I received the police psychologist's monthly billing. I can absolutely confirm that these bills never listed anyone's name, ID number, shift worked, age, or any other possible identifying information whatsoever. The only information was the total number of hours of service rendered and the cost.

I wish I could show you these bills. Not only would they reassure you about confidentiality, but I'm sure you would be just as surprised as I was by how many officers seek professional trauma services. If or when you do, know you are absolutely not alone. In most agencies, the mechanisms for wellness are in place — you just need to use them to recover and heal, so you can continue to be your best for those who love and need you.

Chapter Seven

★

Survival Strategies and Advice

The entire physical world is nothing more than our classroom,
but the challenge to each of us in this classroom is... will you make
choices that enhance your spirit or those that drain your power?
— CAROLINE MYSS

Former San Diego County Sheriff Deputy Mike Spears was involved in a thirteen-minute gunfight in which his two partners were shot and seriously wounded, one critically. Mike didn't receive a scratch from that unbelievable trauma, but he became severely wounded internally from the experience.

Mike describes this experience in a video posted on YouTube (see page 129). Here is part of what he shares about the effects of being an officer and the need to seek help:

> *We're cynical. We see things we don't want to see all the*
> *time. We used to do the job because we loved to do the*
> *job and then we [end up] hating the job because we hate*
> *people, because everybody is an idiot. Eighty percent of*
> *the population that we meet are probably not very good*

people. You get into that mix over and over and over again; it's a broken record, day in and day out. The calls are the same, but they're different. The way that you're looking at them, it's just a call now. You don't want to make that difference. You have to keep making that difference. If you don't make that difference, the job is going to eat you. With every single call, make a difference with that call. Whether it is a kid who crashed on a bike or a homicide scene, whatever it may be, make a difference.

In conversations I've had with Mike, he's shared that he often thinks about how much further he would be in his healing process if he had only known beforehand how essential it is not to isolate himself. How much better off he would be if he'd known how vital it is to remain engaged and active with life, with friends and family, and if he'd known how critical it was to tell his wife earlier what he so desperately needed from her.

While Mike has continued to improve and find ways to work through his trauma, he offers every peace officer this hard-learned advice:

Please don't wait until you're suffering from trauma and posttraumatic stress before you start practicing wellness strategies. They need to become a natural part of your life and service. Enhancing and strengthening resiliency, remaining motivated, processing trauma, and enhancing the quality of your life and service need to be part of your daily routine. Learn from what I have experienced and take your wellness seriously. It's not inevitable that you will suffer from this job, but chances are you will if you don't do anything proactively to enhance your ability to heal, to serve with compassion, and to be at peace.

★ "In an Instant: The Mike Spears Story" ★

In this fifteen-minute video, Officer Mike Spears provides great insights into how trauma has affected him and can impact all officers. He describes the critical incident that changed him, along with other moving examples of trauma he's experienced. Mike gives advice about how to prepare for trauma, how to process it, and how to heal. These are the many simple things that can be part of anyone's daily wellness and resilience practices.

https://www.youtube.com/watch?v=eUHYB7DuMPM
Courtesy of Dan Willis

★

La Mesa Police Officer Tim Purdy

Another powerful example of the impacts of trauma and the ability to heal is La Mesa Police Sergeant Tim Purdy. Tim developed severe posttraumatic stress due to the accumulation of innumerable daily traumas over the course of his twelve-year career, which included several critical incidents, such as a fatal shooting. Eventually, Tim became distant, isolated, and depressed and felt his life was spiraling out of control. He was unable to be or feel normal while being tormented by uncontrollable emotions and terribly distressing thoughts.

All this resulted in serious marital problems. Then the day after Christmas, Tim arrived home from work and discovered his wife had moved out of the house without any notice. Tim had already experienced suicidal thoughts, and this shock literally brought him to his knees, crying uncontrollably for hours in his darkened, empty home. In his great grief and hopeless despair, all he could think about was ending his life. He couldn't see any path forward to recover and heal, and he had no idea what to do in that moment. He was filled with despair over all that he could have and should have done before he reached this desperate and hopeless place.

However, in that worst moment of his life, Tim realized that killing himself would only result in others suffering his loss. He courageously reached for his phone and called a peer-support officer from his agency. That officer, who was off duty, came to his house within twenty minutes and spent the night with him. That gesture literally saved Tim's life.

Tim struggled but sought help from a trauma professional. His department also sent him to the West Coast Post-Trauma Retreat (WCPR), a program in Northern California run by the First Responder Support Network (see Resources) that's specifically for peace officers.

Tim shared his story with me, which he finishes in his own words:

> To this day, that retreat was one of the best gifts I have ever been given. The WCPR is a safe six-day residential treatment center where you attend with other first responders who are suffering from posttraumatic stress, as well as possibly addictions and other issues resulting from our trauma experiences. It was an incredible, lifesaving experience because I was introduced to the

extremely effective posttraumatic stress treatment called EMDR.

EMDR helped me to finally heal from my severe and debilitating internal injuries, which had plagued me for over three years. It helped me to get unstuck, to reboot my brain, and to disassociate myself from all the horrible thoughts and emotions attached to my trauma experience memories, so that I could once again be normal and have my mind function properly. It enabled me to file away in my mind a lot of things and to put them into their proper perspective so that they no longer crippled me. I didn't forget the memories, but with EMDR, I can now think about them and talk about them without suffering any negative or debilitating effects.

Finally, over a year and a half later, I was fully back to loving my life again. I could never have made it without the people who cared for and helped me — the kind and compassionate fellow officers who came to my aid. The department's peer-support team and our police psychologist saved me, and I was once again able to stand up and love the amazing thing we call life.

After about two years, I decided to date again. I found the woman who I truly believe is my soul mate, and we eventually married. I can't express how much I love her and our life now. I am so happy being married to my best friend who understands me, loves me, and is always there.

I have learned also just how important it is to never take anything for granted in this world. But the most important thing I now know is that without good, caring people who will stop and offer emotional support for someone in a time of hurt or loss, the world would have many more terrible tragedies, suicides, and desperate people. I am living proof of that.

You can heal from trauma with treatments such as EMDR and with the caring help and support from others. You can be that lifesaving support for the brothers and sisters you serve with. You do not have to suffer endlessly. Posttraumatic stress injuries do not just go away with time unless you do something helpful to recover. Reach out, get help, and find ways to regain your life. There was that time when I thought it impossible for life to get better. I love life and work now more than ever. So can you.

Self-Awareness Questions

- How familiar are you with the resources available to you through your agency, peer support, chaplain, EAP, and community?
- Does your life partner know of these resources as well?
- Talk with someone in your wellness unit or on your peer-support team, or someone in a position to know, regarding all the resources available to you and your loved ones. Make a list of these resources, and make a plan with your partner for how to use them if needed.

Case Study: Adopting a Learner's Mindset

When eight-year police veteran Sean Smith learns that he has just been passed over to become a detective for the third straight time, he feels disillusioned, angry, and frustrated. All three times he has seen officers with less experience get selected. Feeling resentful of his colleagues and his agency's administration, Officer Smith decides to give up on becoming a detective, thinking it will never happen until he moves to another agency. In the meantime, his disappointment and anger erode his attitude toward his work. He doesn't do as good a job as before, thinking it doesn't matter. But as he gets less out of work, his negativity and bitterness increase — which in turn negatively affects his work relationships, his performance reviews, and any chance of promotion in the future.

Case Study Reflection

In this scenario, Officer Smith chooses to view himself as the "victim" of other people and outside forces. He blames the agency for overlooking him instead of focusing on what he needs to do to become the best candidate. With introspection, he could consider what else he could do to prepare for the testing process and how to improve his work. He could ask those who conducted the testing for specific advice on how to better prepare and improve for next time. He could also speak to several seasoned detectives to find out more about their assignments, learn what they did to prepare to become a detective, and ask their advice. As part of his day-to-day job, Officer Smith could seek advice about his own cases from the department's detectives and their supervisors, just to get to know them better and so they would get to know him. By making the conscious decision to put even more effort into his work, and always trying to do the most complete and thorough investigation in every case, Officer Smith would improve his chances of promotion to detective after the next testing process.

Strategies for Not Taking Work Home

A common dilemma for all peace officers with partners and families is how to avoid taking home the trauma and stress of work so it doesn't negatively affect their loved ones.

In essence, this requires making a conscious break from your hypervigilant work mindset and switching to your caring and trusting personal mindset. Some strategies are to work out or take a run before coming home or as soon as you get home. You can listen to calming, relaxing music on the drive home. You can also stop a few blocks from home and just quietly sit in the car for five minutes. Then do whatever helps you decompress from the workday. Simply think about what you want to do at home; for a few minutes, practice slow, deep breathing; or do a short mindfulness meditation to calm and center yourself.

Envision a dimmer switch inside your brain, and imagine turning the knob from your work mindset to your home mindset. As you take off your peace officer uniform, imagine putting on the "uniform" of the other personal roles in your life — parent, spouse, neighbor, coach, friend, and so on. Once home, establish the routine that your family is to give you some space and leave you alone for fifteen minutes or so. But make sure it is only a short time, and then go out and reconnect with your family.

In addition, once home, choose to do things that keep you active and engaged with others. Don't just come home and vegetate in front of the TV or use alcohol to decompress. Connect with your loved ones through exercise or by playing games, helping with dinner, or any activity everyone enjoys.

There is a good reason why officers struggle to shift mindsets when they come home from work, and why this takes deliberate effort. The hypervigilant work mindset produces adrenaline until we are off duty and leave work, at which point the brain produces biochemicals to rebalance and counteract all the adrenaline in our system. These biochemicals are meant to slow us down, and they tend to leave us feeling tired, low energy, lethargic, disassociated, and "checked out."

After approximately twelve to sixteen hours, the body usually restores its chemical balance and we feel more normal with more energy. But by that time, most officers are back at work and hypervigilant again. The brain is producing more adrenaline, and the subsequent crash after work is harder. As Kevin Gilmartin explains so well in his highly acclaimed book *Emotional Survival for Law Enforcement*, this biochemical roller coaster adversely affects the ability to fall asleep and remain asleep, our mood, our metabolism, our energy level, and our ability to remain active and engaged with life.

That's why it's so important not to take work home, not to work too much overtime, and to do all you can to maintain a healthy life-work balance. That balance requires your full attention and energy, so you keep the emphasis on *life* and not solely on *work*.

---- ★ ----

Conclusion

A career as a peace officer involves sacrifice, giving of oneself, and selfless devotion to protect and enable life. The work is often difficult, and your career will involve countless traumatic assaults upon your spirit, health, and well-being. It takes persistent, *daily* practice of wellness and resilience strategies to strengthen mental, physical, emotional, and spiritual fitness.

The message of this book is one of great hope and promise. Using the tools and strategies it provides, you can take control of your overall wellness, success, and fulfillment in this noble profession.

In the long run, every call matters in the way you choose to handle it. Remain driven with heart-centered service to make a meaningful difference in your agency, with your colleagues, in the community, and with the people you encounter. Respond to traumas and challenges with purposeful intention: Choose to live up to your character in every moment, practice resilience and wellness, and choose to do good and be the good amidst all the bad. Proactively approach every negative situation as a chance to do something positive. Strive to make decisions and take actions that are the most compassionate and life-affirming as possible. See every day and every contact as an opportunity to be useful and helpful and to serve with your heart.

When things get difficult, focus on always being professional; do your job and make a difference when and where you can; and continually take care of yourself and others. The work of a peace officer is, I believe, the greatest job in the world. Get the most out of it. Enjoy it. Love it and all the good that you're able to do. Thank you for your service.

---★---

Notes

Introduction

p. 1 *On average, about 130 officers commit suicide annually*: Christal
Hayes, "'Silence Can Be Deadly': 46 Officers Were Fatally Shot
Last Year. More Than Triple That — 140 — Committed Suicide,"
USA Today, April 11, 2018, https://www.usatoday.com/story
/news/2018/04/11/officers-firefighters-suicides-study
/503735002. These numbers also reflect those reported in the
ongoing research of John M. Violanti, author of *Police Suicide:
Epidemic in Blue* (Springfield, IL: Charles C. Thomas, 2007).

p. 2 *Up to 19 percent of peace officers will suffer*: National Police Support Fund, "Why High Rates of PTSD in Officers?" August 14,
2019, https://nationalpolicesupportfund.com/police-officers
-experience-high-rates-of-ptsd. See also Ellen Kirschman,
"Cops and PTSD," *Psychology Today*, November 30, 2018,
https://www.psychologytoday.com/us/blog/cop-doc/201811
/cops-and-ptsd.

p. 2 *Peace officers are twice as likely to become alcoholics*: Indra
Cidambi, "Police and Addiction," *Psychology Today*, March 30,
2018, https://www.psychologytoday.com/us/blog/sure-recovery
/201803/police-and-addiction.

Chapter Two: The Nine Warning Signs of Trauma

p. 31　*the chances they will commit suicide increase tenfold*: John M. Violanti, "Predictors of Police Suicide Ideation," *Suicide and Life Threatening Behavior* 34, no. 3 (fall 2004): 277–83, https://pubmed.ncbi.nlm.nih.gov/15385182.

p. 31　*At least 20 percent of peace officers will experience*: Indra Cidambi, "Police and Addiction," *Psychology Today*, March 30, 2018, https://www.psychologytoday.com/us/blog/sure-recovery/201803/police-and-addiction.

Chapter Three: Effective Methods to Strengthen Physical, Mental, Spiritual, and Emotional Resilience

p. 40　*it can reduce by 58 percent your chances*: Sheri R. Colberg et al., "Exercise and Type 2 Diabetes," American Diabetes Association, *Diabetes Care* 33, no. 12 (December 2010), https://diabetesjournals.org/care/article/33/12/e147/39268/Exercise-and-Type-2-DiabetesThe-American-College.

p. 40　*After five years spent working patrol, I was selected*: This quote by Angela DeSarro is adapted from Dan Willis, *Bulletproof Spirit: The First Responder's Essential Resource for Protecting and Healing Mind and Heart*, rev. ed. (Novato, CA: New World Library, 2019).

p. 44　*It is within our nature to want to improve, to want something*: This quote by Greg Runge is adapted from *Bulletproof Spirit*.

p. 49　*One of the most popular classes in the long history of Yale University*: David Shimer, "Yale's Most Popular Class Ever: Happiness," January 26, 2018, https://www.nytimes.com/2018/01/26/nyregion/at-yale-class-on-happiness-draws-huge-crowd-laurie-santos.html; and A. Pawlowski, "Yale's Most Popular Class Teaches Happiness: 6 Lessons You Can Practice Now," TODAY.com, February 19, 2018, https://www.today.com/health/yale-popular-happiness-class-6-lessons-you-can-practice-now-t123226.

p. 55　*Science has shown that meditating for just a few minutes*: National Institutes of Health: National Center for Complementary and Integrative Health, "Meditation: In Depth," April 2016, https://www.nccih.nih.gov/health/meditation-in-depth.

p. 57 *A study by Harvard Medical School found that 40 percent*: Shantha M.W. Rajaratnam et al., "Sleep Disorders, Health, and Safety in Police Officers," *Journal of the American Medical Association* 306, no. 23 (December 21, 2011), https://jamanetwork .com/journals/jama/fullarticle/1104746. See also Chuck Remsberg, "Police and Sleep Problems: Are You a 40%er?," *Force Science News*, September 7, 2007, https://www.force science.com/2007/09/police-and-sleep-problems-are-you-a-40er.

Chapter Four: Survival Lessons

p. 66 *The SDPD study was led by Julia Holladay, a researcher for*: Quotes from this unpublished 2011 study are provided with the permission of Julia Holladay, in conjunction with the San Diego Police Department.

Chapter Five: The Spiritual Resilience of Service

p. 89 *In 2017, during an early September morning in Albuquerque*: The details and quotes in this story come from Ed Lavandera, "Police Officer Adopts Homeless Mother's Opioid-Addicted Newborn," CNN, December 3, 2017, https://www.cnn.com /2017/12/01/health/police-officer-adopts-homeless-opioid -newborn-btc-beyond-the-call-of-duty/index.html; and Ed Lavandera, "Stunning Turnaround by a Formerly Addicted Mom Whose Baby Was Adopted by a Police Officer," CNN, July 6, 2018, https://www.cnn.com/2018/07/06/health/police-officer -adopts-baby-addicted-mom-update/index.html.

p. 96 *Serving with your heart and acting with compassion have many*: Heather S. Lonczak, "20 Reasons Why Compassion Is So Important in Psychology," Positive Psychology, June 12, 2021, https://positivepsychology.com/why-is-compassion-important.

p. 101 *"The best and most beautiful things in the world"*: Helen Keller, *The Story of My Life* (New York: Doubleday, Page & Co., 1903), 203.

Chapter Six: Posttraumatic Stress and Ways to Heal

p. 118   *Approximately 25 percent of those experiencing posttraumatic stress*: Jitender Sareen, "Posttraumatic Stress Disorder in Adults: Epidemiology, Pathophysiology, Clinical Manifestations, Course, Assessment, and Diagnosis," UpToDate, September 20, 2021, https://www.uptodate.com/contents/posttraumatic -stress-disorder-in-adults-epidemiology-pathophysiology -clinical-manifestations-course-assessment-and-diagnosis.

p. 118   *Up to 80 percent of people with posttraumatic stress*: Better Health Channel, "Post-traumatic Stress Disorder (PTSD)," February 2, 2017, https://www.betterhealth.vic.gov.au/health /conditionsandtreatments/post-traumatic-stress-disorder-ptsd.

★

Resources

There are numerous resources available to help you safely navigate your career as a peace officer. Below is a list of some of the most effective — from books to websites, call centers, hotlines, and organizations.

In addition, every first responder agency has various resources for you and your immediate family members. This may include an employee assistance program (EAP, which offers free or significantly reduced professional counseling), a peer-support team, chaplains, a wellness unit, or just wellness and peer mentors. Get to know the resources within your agency and let your family know what they are.

Always remember that it's okay to be human. It's okay to be bothered by an experience or event. It's okay to feel hurt, frustrated, angered, anxious, fearful, or saddened. But when you are, seek helpful resources and respond in constructive ways that foster recovery and wellness.

Books

Gilmartin, Kevin M. *Emotional Survival for Law Enforcement: A Guide for Officers and Their Families.* Tucson, AZ: E-S Press, 2002.

Grossman, David, and Loren Christensen. *On Combat: The Psychology and Physiology of Deadly Conflict in War and in Peace*. Mascoutah, IL: Warrior Science Publications, 2008.

Grossman, David, Michael Asken, and Loren Christensen. *Warrior Mindset: Mental Toughness Skills for a Nation's Peacekeepers*. Mascoutah, IL: Human Factor Research Group, 2012.

Kirschman, Ellen. *I Love a Cop: What Police Families Need to Know*. 3rd ed. New York: Guilford Press, 2018.

Shapiro, Francine. *Getting Past Your Past: Take Control of Your Life with Self-Help Techniques from EMDR Therapy*. New York: Rodale, 2013.

Smith, Bobby. *Visions of Courage: The Bobby Smith Story*. Denver, CO: Four Winds Publishing, 2000.

———. *What's in Your Heart Comes out of Your Mouth*. Alexandria, LA: Visions of Courage Publishing, 2013.

———. *The Will to Survive*. Alexandria, LA: Visions of Courage Publishing, 2005.

van der Kolk, Bessel. *The Body Keeps the Score: Brain, Mind, and Body in the Healing of Trauma*. New York: Penguin Books, 2015.

Websites, Hotlines, and Organizations

American Addiction Centers, https://americanaddictioncenters.org /firefighters-first-responders: Addiction resources for any first responder.

Code Green Campaign, http://codegreencampaign.org/resources: Offers an extensive list of crisis resources, both nationwide and in every state.

CopLine, http://copline.org (800-267-5463): Excellent confidential call center staffed solely by well-vetted former officers who are there to listen, support, and provide referrals if desired.

CopsAlive, http://copsalive.com: This Law Enforcement Survival Institute website provides information and strategies to help police officers successfully survive their careers and prepare for the risks that threaten their existence.

Counseling Team International, http://thecounselingteam.com

(800-222-9691): This is an exceptional trauma care and recovery provider that specializes in EMDR treatment.

EMDR International Association, http://emdria.org: Provides information on posttraumatic stress and maintains a nationwide directory of EMDR-trained therapists.

First Responder Support Network, http://frsn.org (415-721-9789): Their mission is to provide treatment programs that promote recovery from stress and critical incidents for first responders and their families.

Institute for Responder Wellness, https://instituteforresponderwellness .com: Provides mental and physical health solutions to first responders and their families, retirees, and providers. They offer training and education to first responders nationwide.

National Law Enforcement Cancer Support Foundation, http://law enforcementcancer.org (888-456-5327): Operated by police officer cancer survivors, this organization offers support and assistance to fellow law-enforcement officers struggling with cancer.

National Police Suicide Foundation, http://psf.org: Provides educational seminars, peer-support strategies, policy and protocol suggestions, and a huge network of resources to survivors and agencies. This is peer support at its very best.

Safe Call Now, http://safecallnowusa.org (206-459-3020): This organization is a confidential resource and call center staffed by retired peace officers.

San Diego Police Department Wellness Unit (main phone: 619-531-2000): Provides information regarding agency wellness programs and officer resilience; officers can call the main number and ask for the Wellness Unit.

West Coast Post-Trauma Retreat, https://frsn.org/west-coast-post -trauma-retreat.html (415-721-9789): Operated by the First Responder Support Network, this six-day program helps first responders heal from trauma, addictions, and other issues (and includes EMDR).

---★---

About the Author

Captain Dan Willis (ret.) is an international instructor in the areas of trauma, posttraumatic stress, and the process of healing. The founder of First Responder Wellness, he provides wellness training to first-responder agencies throughout North America. He also instructs through the International Academy of Public Safety and the National Command and Staff College and was an instructor at the San Diego Police Academy for twelve years.

For nearly thirty years, Captain Willis served as a police officer for the La Mesa Police Department near San Diego, California. He was a homicide, child molestation, sexual assault, and crimes of violence detective for nine years; a SWAT commander; and the developer and coordinator of the police department's wellness program. He graduated from San Diego State University with a bachelor of science degree in criminal justice, and he graduated from the FBI's National Academy for senior police managers in Quantico, Virginia, where he studied wellness and resilience strategies from the FBI's Behavioral Science Unit.

Captain Willis was La Mesa's Officer of the Year twice within four years, was nominated as Detective of the Year for the State of California, and was nominated as Homicide Detective of the Year by the California Homicide Investigators Association.

At the time of this writing, Captain Willis has given over three hundred training presentations in thirty-four states and Canada. He lives in San Diego, California.

For more information, visit firstresponderwellness.com, or contact him via email at dwillis1121@yahoo.com.